Alphabet
Blends and Digraphs

Rigby

Teacher's Guide

Alphabet
Blends and Digraphs

Alphabet Blends and Digraphs Teacher's Guide
part of the Rigby PM Collection

© 1996 Rigby
a division of Reed Elsevier, Inc.
500 Coventry Lane
Crystal Lake, IL. 60014
800-822-8661

Illustrations by Steven D. Mach

00 99
10 9 8 7 6

Printed in Hong Kong by Creative Printing Limited

ISBN 0-7635-2002-0

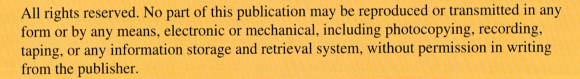

Contents

About the
Alphabet Blends and Digraphs

As children continue to develop as independent readers, they encounter words that are increasingly more difficult to recognize. Once children know how to relate speech sounds to letters in words, they become aware of special combinations of two or three consonants that are represented by a sound formed by blending the individual sounds together. These special letter combinations found in some words are the consonant blends. Furthermore, since English is not a totally phonetic language, children must also become aware of the unique sounds formed by some pairs of letters know as consonant digraphs.

Phonics instruction builds on a child's concept of print and phonemic awareness, or awareness of sounds in spoken words. Good reading instruction addresses the needs of children and provides them with opportunities to:

• develop phonemic awareness through word-play activities, songs, rhymes, tongue twisters, and shared readings of stories and poems.

• explore relationships between sounds and letter combinations in written words.

• explore patterns within words and use that knowledge to decode unknown words.

• build word families to give them access to hundreds of words they can read and write.

• develop word-recognition strategies, such as learning to listen for very fine sound differentiations.

• develop automatic recognition of high-frequency words.

Each *Alphabet Blends and Digraphs* book allows children to focus on one blend or digraph and its letter–sound correspondence. The 32 books in the series give you flexibility of use. By concentrating on the sound of one blend or digraph at a time, children are given the chance to absorb what was learned before moving on to a new letter combination.

Alphabet Blends and Digraphs Books

Each book is titled with the featured blend or digraph.

An alliterative rhyme can be read aloud to children to increase their awareness of the blend or digraph–sound correspondence. Children can then recite the rhyme for pleasure.

A word that begins with the blend or digraph is supported by a colorful photograph that conveys the word's meaning.

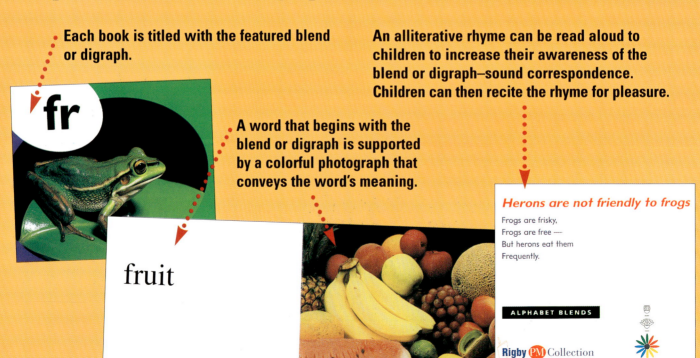

fr

fruit

Herons are not friendly to frogs

Frogs are frisky,
Frogs are free —
But herons eat them
Frequently.

ALPHABET BLENDS

Rigby PM Collection

Alphabet Blends and Digraphs Teacher's Guide

Children hear the sound that a consonant blend or digraph represents in the context of a rhyme, feel the sound as it's made in the mouth, and find objects in the room whose names begin with the letter combination–sound.

Children recognize the blends and digraphs in print and write them within words in small-group and independent learning situations.

Phonics teaching strategies meet the needs of children acquiring English proficiency.

Popular trade books reinforce a phonic element.

Appealing poems, rhymes, songs, and jingles reinforce learning.

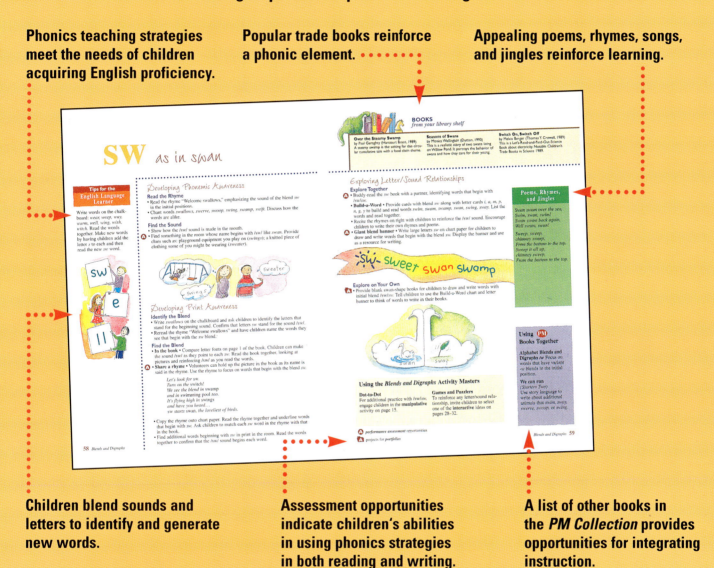

Children blend sounds and letters to identify and generate new words.

Assessment opportunities indicate children's abilities in using phonics strategies in both reading and writing.

A list of other books in the *PM Collection* provides opportunities for integrating instruction.

Alphabet Blends and Digraphs Activity Masters

Reproducible masters provide manipulative and interactive activities that reinforce letter–sound correspondences. The appropriate activity masters are listed for each instructional plan.

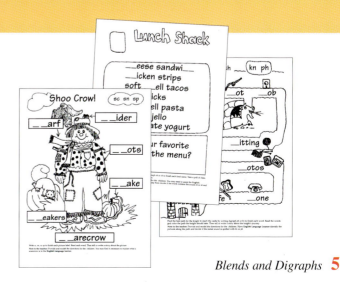

bl as in blueberries

Developing Phonemic Awareness

Read the Rhyme

- Read the rhyme "Blue sky in spring," emphasizing the sound of the blend *bl* in the initial positions.
- Chant words *blustery, blowing, black, blue, blossoms.* Discuss how the words are alike.

Find the Sound

- Show how the /bl/ sound is made in the mouth.
- (A) Find something in the room whose name begins with /bl/ like *blustery.* Provide clues such as: wooden shapes to build with (*blocks*); a crayon the color of the sky (*blue*).

Developing Print Awareness

Identify the Blend

- Write *blue* on the chalkboard and ask children to identify the letters that stand for the beginning sound. Confirm that letters *bl* stand for the sound /bl/.
- Reread the rhyme "Blue sky in spring" and have children name the words they see that begin with the *bl* blend.

Find the Blend

- **In the book** • Make the sound /bl/ as the letters *bl* are traced on page 1 of the book. Read the book together, looking at pictures and reinforcing /bl/ as you read the words.
- (A) • **Share a rhyme** • Volunteers can hold up the picture in the book as its name is said in the rhyme. Use the rhyme to focus on words that begin with the blend *bl.*

    Bl *is for* blood *when I fell and cut my knee;*
    Bl *is for the* blanket *I use to cover me.*
    Bl *is for the colors* black *and* blue;
    Blueberries *start with the letters* bl *too.*

- Copy the rhyme onto chart paper. Read the rhyme together and underline words that begin with *bl.* Ask children to match each *bl* word in the rhyme with that in the book.
- Find additional words beginning with *bl* in print in the room. Read the words together to confirm that the /bl/ sound begins each word.

BOOKS
from your library shelf

Blueberries for Sal
by Robert McCloskey (Puffin, 1976)
A girl named Sal goes blueberry picking with her mother and meets with a family of black bears who are doing the same.

Black Crow, Black Crow
by Ginger Foglesong Guy (Greenwillow, 1991) This book uses rhythmic language to tell the story of a busy mother crow and her brood.

Blackberry Ramble
by Thacher Hurd (Philomel, 1990)
While the mouse family is trying to do spring cleaning, baby Mouse is just "noodling around" and ends up falling into a blackberry pie.

Exploring Letter/Sound Relationships

Explore Together

 • Buddy-read the *bl* book with a partner, identifying words that begin with /bl/*bl*.
• **Build-a-Word** • Provide cards with blend *bl* along with letter cards *a, e, i, o, c, k, n, t, d* to build and read words *black, blank, blanket, blend, blind, blink, block, blond, blot*. List the words and read together.

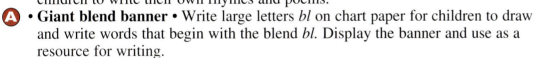

• Recite the rhymes on right with children to reinforce the /bl/ sound. Encourage children to write their own rhymes and poems.
 • **Giant blend banner** • Write large letters *bl* on chart paper for children to draw and write words that begin with the blend *bl*. Display the banner and use as a resource for writing.

Explore on Your Own

 • Provide blank black construction paper books for children to use a white crayon to draw and write words with initial blend /bl/*bl*. Tell children to use the Build-a-Word chart and blend banner to think of words to write in their books.

Poems, Rhymes, and Jingles

Blanche's blackberries bloomed and blossomed.

A blinding blowing blizzard blocked the roads.

*Cold and raw the north wind doth blow,
Bleak in the morning early;
A blizzard has covered the hills with snow,
And winter's now come fairly.*

Using **PM** Books Together

Alphabet Blends and Digraphs *cl, fl, gl, pl, sl*
Focus on words that have a variety of blends with *-l* in the initial position.

Go-carts
(Starters One)
Design a black go-cart to add to the story and write a sentence about it.

Using the *Blends and Digraphs* Activity Masters

The Clock Shop *and* Mixed-Up Letters
For additional practice with /bl/*bl*, engage children in the **manipulative** activities on pages 9 and 11.

Games and Puzzlers
To reinforce any letter/sound relationship, invite children to select one of the **interactive** ideas on pages 29–32.

 performance assessment opportunities

 projects for *portfolios*

br as in bread

Tips for the English Language Learner

Make three columns on the chalkboard with heads *b, r, br.* Write known words under each heading: *books, bears, red, river, brush, bricks.* [See *Alphabet Starters b, r.*] Give each child letter cards for *b* and *r.* Say words that begin with *b, r,* or *br.* The child holds up one or both letter cards to show the beginning letter(s). Write the word in the column. Read the words and underline the letter(s) that represents the initial sound.

Developing Phonemic Awareness

Read the Rhyme
- Read the rhyme "The brand new bridge," emphasizing the sound of the blend *br* in the initial positions.
- Chant words *brand, bridge, brown, broken* . Discuss how the words are alike.

Find the Sound
- Show how the /br/ sound is made in the mouth.
- Ⓐ Find something in the room whose name begins with /br/ like *bridge.* Provide clues such as: something to sweep with (*broom*); a crayon the color of chocolate (*brown*).

Developing Print Awareness

Identify the Blend
- Write *brown bridge* on the chalkboard and ask children to identify the letters that stand for the beginning sound. Confirm that letters *br* stand for the sound /br/.
- Reread the rhyme "The brand new bridge" and have children name the words they see that begin with the *br* blend.

Find the Blend
- **In the book** • Make the sound /br/ as the letters *br* are traced on page 1 of the book. Read the book together, looking at pictures and reinforcing /br/ as you read the words.
- Ⓐ **Share a rhyme** • Volunteers can hold up the picture in the book as its name is said in the rhyme. Use the rhyme to focus on words that begin with the blend *br*:

  If you're painting a wall or grooming your hair,
  you need… brushes!
  If you're traveling over water and need to get from here to there,
  you need a… bridge!
  If you're building a house and want to make it last,
  you need… bricks!
  If you're hungry and want a snack fast,
  you need some… bread!
  If you mix green and red, what color have you instead? Brown!

- Copy the rhyme onto chart paper. Read the rhyme together and underline words that begin with *br.* Ask children to match each *br* word in the rhyme with that in the book.
- Find additional words beginning with *br* in print in the room. Read the words together to confirm that the /br/ sound begins each word.

BOOKS
from your library shelf

The Brave Little Tailor
retold by Peggy Thompson (Simon & Schuster, 1992)
This brave little tailor marries a princess, conquers a giant, and improves his lot.

A Brown Cow
by Bijou LeTord (Little, Brown, 1989)
With childlike style, a little girl describes a little brown cow that lives in her yard.

The Bridge
by Emily Cheney Neville (Harper & Row, 1988)
Little Ben watches the big machines as a new bridge is built near his home.

Exploring Letter/Sound Relationships

Explore Together

(A) • Buddy-read the *br* book with a partner, identifying words that begin with /br/*br*.

• **Word puzzlers** • Display cards with words *breakfast, bran, branch, bricks, bread, brakes, brain, break, bridge, brush*. Provide the following clues for children to find and identify each word: limb of a tree; used to build houses; used to stop a bike; used for making sandwiches; kind of a cereal; first meal of the day; smash into pieces; part of the body used for thinking; something to paint with; a way to travel over water.

• Recite the rhymes on right with children to reinforce the /br/ sound. Encourage children to write their own rhymes and poems.

(A) • **Giant blend banner** • Write large letters *br* on chart paper for children to draw and write words that begin with the blend *br*. Display the banner and use as a resource for writing.

Explore on Your Own

(A) • Provide paints, brushes, and large sheets of art paper for children to paint words that begin with *br*. Tell children to use the blend banner to think of words to write in their books.

Poems, Rhymes, and Jingles

Brad brought brown bran bread for breakfast.

Brenda broke her brand new braided bracelet.

*There was a brave woman tossed up in a basket,
Seventeen times
as high as the moon;
Where she was going
I couldn't but ask it,
For in her hand
she carried a broom.*

Using (PM) Books Together

Alphabet Blends and Digraphs *cr, dr, fr, gr, pr, tr* Focus on words that have a variety of -r blends in the initial position.

In the shopping cart
(Starters One)
Write additional sentences for the story using food names that begin with /br/*br*.

Using the *Blends and Digraphs* Activity Masters

Hidden Pictures *and* Pretty Presents
For additional practice with /br/*br*, engage children in the **manipulative** activities on pages 7 and 8.

Games and Puzzlers
To reinforce any letter/sound relationship, invite children to select one of the **interactive** ideas on pages 29–32.

 performance assessment opportunities

 projects for *portfolios*

ch as in cherries

Tips for the English Language Learner

Write words on the chalkboard: *hip, win, leap, voice, wild, rain, few, heat, walk.* Read the words with children. Change the initial letter in each word and write a new word with *ch* next to the word on the board. Read the rhyming word pairs.

Developing Phonemic Awareness

Read the Rhyme
- Read the rhyme "Cheetahs," emphasizing the sound of the digraph *ch* in the initial positions.
- Chant words *cheetahs, champions, chasing.* Discuss how the words are alike.

Find the Sound
- Show how the /ch/ sound is made in the mouth.
- **Ⓐ** Find something in the room whose name begins with /ch/ like *cheetahs.* Provide clues such as: something you sit on (*chair*); something you use to write on the chalkboard (*chalk*).

Developing Print Awareness

Identify the Digraph
- Write *cheetah* on the chalkboard and ask children to identify the letters that stand for the beginning sound. Confirm that letters *ch* stand for the sound /ch/.
- Reread the rhyme "Cheetahs" and have children name the words they see that begin with the digraph *ch.*

Find the Digraph
- **In the book** • Make the sound /ch/ as the letters *ch* are traced on page 1 of the book. Read the book together, looking at pictures and emphasizing /ch/ as you read the words.
- **Ⓐ** **Share a rhyme** • Volunteers can hold up the picture in the book as its name is said in the rhyme. Use the rhyme to focus on words that begin with the digraph *ch.*

  > Ch *starts many words…*
  > children *for playing,*
  > chairs *for sitting,*
  > chimneys *for heating,*
  > cherries *for eating,*
  > chains *for fastening.*

- Copy the rhyme onto chart paper. Read the rhyme together and underline words that begin with *ch.* Ask children to match each *ch* word in the rhyme with that in the book.
- Find additional words beginning with *ch* in print in the room. Read the words together to confirm that the /ch/ sound begins each word.

BOOKS
from your library shelf

Chicka Chicka Boom Boom
by Bill Martin, Jr., and John Archambault (Simon & Schuster, 1989)
Children will enjoy the word play and repetition in this rhyme about an active alphabet.

Chicken Sunday
by Patricia Polacco (G. P. Putnam's, 1992)
Ch is definitely for fried chicken on Sunday for Miss Eula Mae Walker's family.

Arthur's Chicken Pox
by Marc Brown (Little, Brown, 1994)
Another funny episode in the life of Arthur Aardvark, who catches chicken pox.

Chicken Little
by Steven Kellogg (William Morrow, 1985)
Visual jokes, puns, and silly details give new life to this old tale.

Exploring Letter/Sound Relationships

Explore Together

- (A) Buddy-read the *ch* book with a partner, identifying words that begin with /ch/*ch.*
- **Build-a-Word** • Provide cards with digraph *ch* along with letter cards *e, a, i, r, n, t, l, d* to build and read words *chair, chain, chart, chat, cheat, child, chin.* List the words and read together.
- (A) **Giant digraph banner** • Write large letters *ch* on chart paper for children to draw and write words that begin with the digraph *ch.* Display the banner and use as a resource for writing.
- Recite the rhymes on right with children to reinforce the /ch/ sound. Encourage children to write their own rhymes and poems.

Explore on Your Own

- (A) Provide construction paper strips for children to write words with initial digraph *ch* to make a word chain. Tell children to use the Build-a-Word chart and digraph banner to think of words to write on their chains.

Poems, Rhymes, and Jingles

Chester chomps chili cheeseburgers.

Cheerful chipmunks chew chestnuts.

Chook chook
chook chook chook.
Good morning, Mrs. Hen.
How many chickens
have you got?
She cheered, "I've got ten!
Four of them are yellow,
And four are chocolate
brown,
And two of them are
cherry red,
The choicest in the town!"

Using the *Blends and Digraphs* Activity Masters

Chicken Letters, Lunch Shack, *and* Digraph Dominos
For additional practice with /ch/*ch,* engage children in the **manipulative** activities on pages 17, 18, 22–23.

Games and Puzzlers
To reinforce any letter/sound relationship, invite children to select one of the **interactive** ideas on pages 29–32.

Using PM Books Together

Alphabet Blends and Digraphs *wh, th, ph, sh*
Focus on words that have a variety of digraphs in the initial position.

We can run
(Starters Two)
Read about other fast-moving animals. Write a sentence about the *cheetah.*

(A) ***performance assessment*** opportunities
(A) projects for ***portfolios***

cl as in clothes

Developing Phonemic Awareness

Read the Rhyme

- "The cliff climbing class," emphasizing the sound of the blend *cl* in the initial positions.
- Chant words *cliff, climbing, class, climbers, climb, clamber, clinging, closely*. Discuss how the words are alike.

Find the Sound

- Show how the /kl/ sound is made in the mouth.
- **(A)** Find something in the room whose name begins with /kl/ like *cliff climbing class*.
- Provide clues such as: something to tell the time (*clock*); something everyone is wearing (*clothes*).

Developing Print Awareness

Identify the Blend

- Write *class* on the chalkboard and ask children to identify the letters that stand for the beginning sound. Confirm that letters *cl* stand for the sound /kl/.
- Reread the rhyme "The cliff climbing class" and have children name the words they see that begin with the *cl* blend.

Find the Blend

- **In the book** • Make the sound /kl/ as the letters *cl* are traced on page 1 of the book. Read the book together, looking at pictures and emphasizing /kl/ as you read the words.
- **(A)** • **Share a rhyme** • Volunteers can hold up the picture in the book as its name is said in the rhyme. Use the rhyme to focus on words that begin with the blend *cl*.

> Cl *is for* clothes
> *and* clouds *in the sky,*
> *the* claws *on a bird*
> *as it soars way up high;*
> Cl *is for* clock.
> *It's time for the show!*
> *Here comes the circus* clown
> *with silly hat and big bow!*

- Copy the rhyme onto chart paper. Read the rhyme together and underline words that begin with *cl*. Ask children to match each *cl* word in the rhyme with that in the book.
- Find additional words beginning with *cl* in print in the room. Read the words together to confirm that the /kl/ sound begins each word.

BOOKS
from your library shelf

Clifford the Firehouse Dog
by Norman Bridwell (Scholastic, 1994)
The big red dog tries to do the right thing, but he does make mistakes. Another book in the series of ever-popular Clifford, the big red dog.

Clap Your Hands
by Lorinda Bryan Cauley
(G. P. Putnam's, 1992)
In this rollicking rhyme children will want to clap their hands and perform all the other actions while reciting the words.

Clowning Around
by Cathryn Falwell (Orchard Books, 1991)
A red-and-white polka-dot clown rearranges letters to make words to read. Children may want to use letter cards to do some clowning around on their own.

Exploring Letter/Sound Relationships

Explore Together

Ⓐ • Buddy-read the *cl* book with a partner, identifying words that begin with /kl/*cl*.
• **Build-a-Word** • Provide cards with blend *cl* along with letter cards *a, p, m, y, w, i* to build and read words *clap, clam, clay, clamp, claw, clip*. List the words and read together.
• Recite the rhymes on right with children to reinforce the /kl/ sound. Encourage children to write their own rhymes and poems.
Ⓐ • **Giant blend banner** • Write large letters *cl* on chart paper for children to draw and write words that begin with the blend *cl*. Display the banner and use as a resource for writing.

Explore on Your Own

Ⓐ • Provide blank cloud-shape books for children to draw and write words with initial blend /kl/*cl*. Tell children to use the Build-a-Word chart and blend banner to think of words to write in their books.

Poems, Rhymes, and Jingles

*The class clapped
as the clumsy clown
fell in a clump of clover.*

*Clear the clutter and
clean the classroom.*

*Clickety-clack,
clickety-clack,
The train clanged
down the track.
Clickety-clack,
clickety-clack.*

Using Ⓟⓜ Books Together

Alphabet Blends and Digraphs *bl, fl, gl, pl, sl* Focus on words that have a variety of initial *-l* blends.

Climbing *(Starters One)* Write sentences telling about real and make-believe places you can climb. Use words that begin with *cl*.

Using the *Blends and Digraphs* Activity Masters

The Clock Shop *and* Mixed-Up Letters
For additional practice with /kl/*cl*, engage children in the **manipulative** activities on pages 9 and 11.

Games and Puzzlers
To reinforce any letter/sound relationship, invite children to select one of the **interactive** ideas on pages 29–32.

Ⓐ *performance assessment* opportunities

 projects for *portfolios*

cr as in crown

Tips for the English Language Learner

Make three columns on the chalkboard with heads *c, r, cr.* Write known words under each heading: *cake, cup, red, road, crab, crown.* [See *Alphabet Starters c, r.*] Give each child letter cards for *c* and *r.* Say words that begin with *c, r,* or *cr.* The child holds up one or both letter cards to show the beginning letter(s). Write the word in the column. Read the words and underline the letter(s) that represents the initial sound.

Developing Phonemic Awareness

Read the Rhyme
- Read the rhyme "Crawling crab," emphasizing the sound of the blend *cr* in the initial positions.
- Chant words *crawling, crab, crusty, crawls, creeps, crack, crooked.* Discuss how the words are alike.

Find the Sound
- Show how the /kr/ sound is made in the mouth.
- **(A)** Find something in the room whose name begins with /kr/ like *crawling crab.* Provide clues such as: something to color with (*crayon*); the outside edge of your sandwich bread (*crust*).

Developing Print Awareness

Identify the Blend
- Write *crab* on the chalkboard and ask children to identify the letters that stand for the beginning sound. Confirm that letters *cr* stand for the sound /kr/.
- Reread the rhyme "Crawling crab" and have children name the words they see that begin with the *cr* blend. As one group recites the rhyme, the others can creep about the room as crabs. Then switch roles.

Find the Blend
- **In the book** • Make the sound /kr/ as the letters *cr* are traced on page 1 of the book. Read the book together, looking at pictures and emphasizing /kr/ as you read the words.
- **(A)** **Share a rhyme** • Volunteers can hold up the picture in the book as its name is said in the rhyme. Use the rhyme to focus on words that begin with the blend *cr.*

> Cr *is for* crane *and for* crocodile *too.*
> *If one came your way, what would you do?*
> Cr *is for a* crown *of gold for a king to wear*
> *and for a box of* crayons *for children to share.*
> *Here comes one more* cr *word, its name is* crab, *you know.*
> *Because the crab has eight legs, it's always on the go.*

- Copy the rhyme onto chart paper. Read the rhyme together and underline words that begin with *cr.* Ask children to match each *cr* word in the rhyme with that in the book.
- Find additional words beginning with *cr* in print in the room. Read the words together to confirm that the /kr/ sound begins each word.

BOOKS
from your library shelf

Crazy Alphabet
by Lynn Cox (Orchard, 1990)
In this cumulative tale, alphabet sentences build on a repetitive pattern. Colorful pages show a crazy quilt collage of shapes and patterns.

Crocodile Beat
by Gail Jergensen (Bradbury Press, 1989)
Sing-song text tells about a crowd of active animals dancing and playing and stomping their feet. Lots of words with blends.

The Crow and Mrs. Gaddy
by Wilson Gage (Greenwillow, 1984)
Children will laugh at the hilarious attempts of the crow and Mrs. Gaddy's retaliation.

Exploring Letter/Sound Relationships

Explore Together

A • Buddy-read the *cr* book with a partner, identifying words that begin with /kr/*cr*.

• **Build-a-Word** • Provide cards with blend *cr* along with letter cards *a, b, y, i, o, w, n* to build and read words *crab, cry, crib, crow, crown, crowd*. List the words and read together.

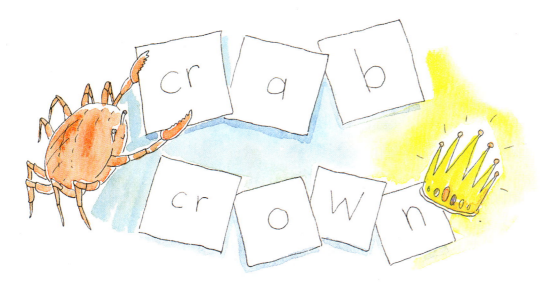

• Recite the rhymes on right with children to reinforce the /kr/ sound. Encourage children to write their own rhymes and poems.

A • **Giant blend banner** • Write large letters *cr* on chart paper for children to draw and write words that begin with the blend *cr*. Display the banner and use as a resource for writing.

Explore on Your Own

A • Provide blank crayon-shape books for children to draw and write words with initial blend /kr/*cr*. Tell children to use the blend banner to think of words to write in their books.

Poems, Rhymes, and Jingles

Crooked crawling creepy crickets crawl across the carpet.

Cranky Craig Crocodile crunches cracker-coated crabcakes.

*Crick-crack, wind at my back.
My hat flew off and won't come back.*

Using **PM** Books Together

Alphabet Blends and Digraphs *br, dr, fr, gr, pr, tr* Focus on words that have a variety of *-r* blends in the initial position.

The rock pools
(Starters Two)
Visit crabs in their natural habitat. Identify other sea creatures whose names begin or end with blends and digraphs: *shells, shrimps, starfish, fish.*

Using the *Blends and Digraphs* Activity Masters

Story Time *and* Pretty Presents
For additional practice with /kr/*cr*, engage children in the **manipulative** activities on pages 6 and 8.

Games and Puzzlers
To reinforce any letter/sound relationship, invite children to select one of the **interactive** ideas on pages 29–32.

 performance assessment opportunities

 projects for *portfolios*

dr *as in drum*

Developing Phonemic Awareness

Read the Rhyme

- Read the rhyme "Drawing," emphasizing the sound of the blend *dr* in the initial positions.
- Chant words *drawing, drawn, drawbridge, dreadful, dragon.* Discuss how the words are alike.

Find the Sound

- Show how the /dr/ sound is made in the mouth.
- **(A)** Find something in the room whose name begins with /dr/ like *dreadful dragon.* Provide clues such as: change the beginning sound in *mess* to /dr/ and what do you have? (*dress*); change the beginning sound in *hum* to /dr/ and what do you have? (*drum*)

Developing Print Awareness

Identify the Blend

- Write *dreadful dragon* on the chalkboard and ask children to identify the letters that stand for the beginning sound. Confirm that letters *dr* stand for the sound /dr/.
- Reread the rhyme "Drawing" and have children name the words they see that begin with the *dr* blend.

Find the Blend

- **In the book** • Make the sound /dr/ as the letters *dr* are traced on page 1 of the book. Read the book together, looking at pictures and emphasizing /dr/ as you read the words.
- **(A)** • **Share a rhyme** • Volunteers can hold up the picture in the book as its name is said in the rhyme. Use the rhyme to focus on words that begin with the blend *dr.*

  > Dr *is for* drain *and the* drum *that I beat.*
  > Dr *is for my* drawer *that I cannot keep neat.*
  > Dr *is for* drawing *pictures real and make-believe,*
  > *like a* dragon *that spurts fire whenever it breathes.*

- Copy the rhyme onto chart paper. Read the rhyme together and underline words that begin with *dr.* Ask children to match each *dr* word in the rhyme with that in the book.
- Find additional words beginning with *dr* in print in the room. Read the words together to confirm that the /dr/ sound begins each word.

Dragon
by Wayne Anderson
(Simon & Schuster, 1992)
An egg drops from the sky, and the newborn dragon goes in search of his mother. [A good book to read to children].

Draw Me a Star
by Eric Carle (Philomel, 1992)
This is a circular story about a boy painting at his easel. He draws a star and then one picture leads to another, ending at the star.

The Dragon Nanny
by C.L.G. Martin (Macmillan, 1988)
Nanny Nell Hannah is fired by the king and ends up being nanny to two baby dragons. Children's Choice.

Exploring Letter/Sound Relationships

Explore Together

A • Buddy-read the *dr* book with a partner, identifying words that begin with /dr/*dr*.

• **Build-a-Word** • Provide cards with blend *dr* along with letter cards *a, e, g, w, n, k, p, y* to build and read words *drag, draw, drain, drink, drank, drip, dry*. List the words and read together. Use words in sentences about a dragon.

• Recite the rhymes on right with children to reinforce the /dr/ sound. Encourage children to write their own rhymes and poems.

A • **Giant blend banner** • Write large letters *dr* on chart paper for children to draw and write words that begin with the blend *dr*. Display the banner and use as a resource for writing.

Explore on Your Own

A • Provide blank drum-shape books for children to draw and write words with initial blend *dr*. Tell children to use the Build-a-Word chart and blend banner to think of words to write in their books.

draw   drink

Using the *Blends and Digraphs* Activity Masters

Story Time *and* Pretty Presents
For additional practice with /dr/*dr*, engage children in the **manipulative** activities on pages 6 and 8.

Games and Puzzlers
To reinforce any letter/sound relationship, invite children to select one of the **interactive** ideas on pages 29–32.

Poems, Rhymes, and Jingles

The dreadful dragon stood on the drawbridge and drank the river dry.

Drew draws dromedaries dressed in dresses.

*Little Bo-Peep has lost her sheep
And doesn't know where to find them.
Leave them alone, and they'll come home,
Dragging their tails behind them.*

Using **PM** **Books Together**

Alphabet Blends and Digraphs *br, cr, gr, pr, tr*
Focus on words that have a variety of *-r* blends in the initial position.

The pencil
(*Starters Two*)
Partners may enjoy teaching one another how to draw a special shape or animal.

 performance assessment opportunities

 projects for *portfolios*

fl as in flag

Tips for the
English Language Learner

If children are having difficulty blending *f* and *l*, provide a list of words on the chalkboard to read: *lag, lake, lame, lap, lash, led, lick, lip, lit, lock, low.* The child can make new words by adding letter *f: flag, flake, flame, flap, flash, fled, flick, flip, flit, flock, flow.* Read the words together.

Developing Phonemic Awareness

Read the Rhyme
• Read the rhyme "Flying in the wind," emphasizing the sound of the blend *fl* in the initial positions.
• Chant words *flying, flags, flap, flames, flare, fly.* Discuss how the words are alike.

Find the Sound
• Show how the /fl/ sound is made in the mouth.
A • Find something in the room whose name begins with /fl/ like *flags flying.* Provide clues such as: change the beginning sound in *door* to *fl* and what do you have? (*floor*); change the beginning sound in *shower* to *fl* and what do you have? (*flower*)

Developing Print Awareness

Identify the Blend
• Write *flag* on the chalkboard and ask children to identify the letters that stand for the beginning sound. Confirm that letters *fl* stand for the sound /fl/.
• Reread the rhyme "Flying in the wind" and have children name the words they see that begin with the *fl* blend.

Find the Blend
• **In the book** • Make the sound /fl/ as the letters *fl* are traced on page 1 of the book. Read the book together, looking at pictures and emphasizing /fl/ as you read the words.
A • **Share a rhyme** • Volunteers can hold up the picture in the book as its name is said in the rhyme. Use the rhyme to focus on words that begin with the blend *fl.*

> Fl *is for* flood *waters and the* fly *that's buzzing by.*
> *Look up and you will see a* flag *waving at the sky.*
> *Look down at* fl *on the* floor; *sweep to keep it clean.*
> Fl *is for this bunch of* flowers, *the prettiest I have seen.*

• Copy the rhyme onto chart paper. Read the rhyme together and underline words that begin with *fl.* Ask children to match each *fl* word in the rhyme with that in the book.
• Find additional words beginning with *fl* in print in the room. Read the words together to confirm that the /fl/ sound begins each word.

BOOKS
from your library shelf

Flap Your Wings and Try
by Charlotte Pomerantz
(Greenwillow, 1989)
A bird learning to fly is repeatedly told to "flap your wings and try."

Flossie and the Fox
by Patricia McKissack (Dial, 1986)
Flossie is on an errand to deliver eggs when she must outwit a sly fox. Notable Children's Trade Book in the Language Arts.

When the Fly Flew In . . .
by Lisa Westberg Peters (Dial, 1994)
A pesty fly comes in and disturbs a dog, a parakeet, and a cat.

Exploring Letter/Sound Relationships

Explore Together

Ⓐ • Buddy-read the *fl* book with a partner, identifying words that begin with /fl/*fl*.
• **Build-a-Word** • Provide cards with blend *fl* along with letter cards *a, i, o, e, g, k, m, p, t* to build and read words *flag, flake, flame, flap, flat, flip, float*. List the words and read together.
• Recite the rhymes on right with children to reinforce the /fl/ sound. Encourage children to write their own rhymes and poems.
Ⓐ • **Giant blend banner** • Write large letters *fl* on chart paper for children to draw and write words that begin with the blend *fl*. Display the banner and use as a resource for writing.

Explore on Your Own

Ⓐ • Provide sheets of flannel or paper for children to write words with initial blend *fl* to make a flag. Attach a drinking straw or stick to finish each flag. Tell children to use the Build-a-Word chart and blend banner to think of words to write in their books.

Using the *Blends and Digraphs* Activity Masters

The Clock Shop *and* Mixed-Up Letters
For additional practice with /fl/*fl*, engage children in the **manipulative** activities on pages 9 and 11.

Games and Puzzlers
To reinforce any letter/sound relationship, invite children to select one of the **interactive** ideas on pages 29–32.

Using Ⓟ︎Ⓜ︎ Books Together

Alphabet Blends and Digraphs *bl, cl, gl, pl, sl*
Focus on words that have a variety of -*l* blends in the initial position.

Can you see the eggs?
(Starters Two)
Which animal lays eggs in a flower? Share other flower facts.

 performance assessment opportunities

 projects for *portfolios*

fr as in frog

Tips for the English Language Learner

Help children understand how sounds are blended together and how leaving out a letter or adding a letter changes a word. Use letter cards to build words: *frog, free, frame, fright, frail.* Then ask the child: What would frog be without the *r*? (*fog*); free? (*fee*); frame? (*fame*); fright? (*fight*); frail? (*fail*). Add the *r* again and read the original words.

Developing Phonemic Awareness

Read the Rhyme
- Read the rhyme "Herons are not friendly to frogs," emphasizing the sound of the blend *fr* in the initial positions.
- Chant words *friendly, frogs, frisky, free, frequently.* Discuss how the words are alike.

Find the Sound
- Show how the /fr/ sound is made in the mouth.
- Find something in the room whose name begins with /fr/ like *frisky frogs.* Provide clues such as: Change the beginning sound in *send* to /fr/ and who do you have? (*friend*) Change the beginning sound in *lost* to /fr/ and what do you have? (*frost*)

Developing Print Awareness

Identify the Blend
- Write *frisky frogs* on the chalkboard and ask children to identify the letters that stand for the beginning sound. Confirm that letters *fr* stand for the sound /fr/.
- Reread the rhyme "Herons are not friendly to frogs" and have children name the words they see that begin with the *fr* blend. One group can read as another moves about like frogs. Then switch roles.

Find the Blend
- **In the book** • Make the sound /fr/ as the letters *fr* are traced on page 1 of the book. Read the book together, looking at pictures and emphasizing /fr/ as you read the words.
- **Share a rhyme** • Volunteers can hold up the picture in the book as its name is said in the rhyme. Use the rhyme to focus on words that begin with the blend *fr.*

> Fr *is in your kitchen*
> *in* fruit *and* frying *pan.*
> Fr *is for a little* frog—
> *catch one, if you can!*
> *Look at any wooden* frame;
> Fr *is in it too.*
> *Do you have* freckles
> *on your face and arms?*
> *Then* fr *is on you too!*

- Copy the rhyme onto chart paper. Read the rhyme together and underline words that begin with *fr.* Ask children to match each *fr* word in the rhyme with that in the book.
- Find additional words beginning with *fr* in print in the room. Read the words together to confirm that the /fr/ sound begins each word.

Frog Went a-Courting
by Wendy Watson
(Lothrop, Lee & Shepard, 1990)
This folksong is an account of the courtship and wedding of a mouse and frog.

Frogs
by Graham Tarrant (G. P. Putnam's, 1983)
This three-dimensional pop-up book shows the stages of frog development. Children's Choices.

Frida's Office Day
by Thomas P. Lewis (Harper & Row, 1989)
Enjoy a day with Frida while focusing on lots of words with *fr, tr, ph ,fl.*

Exploring Letter/Sound Relationships

Explore Together

Ⓐ • Buddy-read the *fr* book with a partner, identifying words that begin with /fr/*fr.*
• **Build-a-Word** • Provide cards with blend *fr* along with letter cards *o, m, n, t, s, z, e, y, w* to build and read words *from, front, frost, frown, froze, fry.* List the words and read together.
• Recite the rhymes on right with children to reinforce the /fr/ sound. Encourage children to write their own rhymes and poems.

Ⓐ • **Giant blend banner** • Write large letters *fr* on chart paper for children to draw and write words that begin with the blend *fr.* Display the banner and use as a resource for writing.

Explore on Your Own

Ⓐ • Provide blank frog-shape books for children to draw and write words with initial blend /fr/*fr.* Tell children to use the Build-a-Word chart and blend banner to think of words to write in their books.

Poems, Rhymes, and Jingles

Frank's friend Fran freezes fresh fruit.

Frisky frogs frequently frolic in the fields.

One frigid frosty morning When freezing was the weather, I met a frail old man Clothed all in leather.

Using Ⓟⓜ Books Together

Alphabet Blends and Digraphs *br, cr, dr, gr, pr, tr* Focus on words that have a variety of -*r* blends in the initial position.

Where are the babies?
(Starters Two)
Take a look at mother frog and her babies in their natural habitat.

Using the *Blends and Digraphs* Activity Masters

Story Time *and* Pretty Presents
For additional practice with /fr/*fr,* engage children in the **manipulative** activities on pages 6 and 8.

Games and Puzzlers
To reinforce any letter/sound relationship, invite children to select one of the **interactive** ideas on pages 29–32.

 performance assessment opportunities

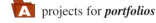 projects for *portfolios*

gl as in gloves

Children can change the beginning sound in each of the following words to /gl/ and say the new word. Write the words children say, read the words together, and talk about how they are alike. Say words: *had, new, low, love, robe, pass, hide.*

Developing Phonemic Awareness

Read the Rhyme
• Read the rhyme "Dark glasses stop glare," emphasizing the sound of the blend *gl* in the initial positions.
• Chant words *glasses, glare, glistens, glitters, glares.* Discuss how the words are alike.

Find the Sound
• Show how the /gl/ sound is made in the mouth.
(A) • Find something in the room whose name begins with /gl/ like *glasses.* Provide clues such as: a round ball with a map of the world on it (*globe*); something you wear on your hands to keep them warm (*gloves*).

Developing Print Awareness

Identify the Blend
• Write *glasses* on the chalkboard and ask children to identify the letters that stand for the beginning sound. Confirm that letters *gl* stand for the sound /gl/.
• Reread the rhyme "Dark glasses stop glare" and have children name the words they see that begin with the *gl* blend.

Find the Blend
• **In the book** • Make the sound /gl/ as the letters *gl* are traced on page 1 of the book. Read the book together, looking at pictures and reinforcing /gl/ as you read the words.
(A) • **Share a rhyme** • Volunteers can hold up the picture in the book as its name is said in the rhyme. Use the rhyme to focus on words that begin with the blend *gl.*

> Glue *is for sticking;*
> Glass *is for sipping;*
> Gloves *are for warming;*
> Glasses *are for seeing;*
> Glider *is for flying.*

• Copy the rhyme onto chart paper. Read the rhyme together and underline words that begin with *gl.* Ask children to match each *gl* word in the rhyme with that in the book.
• Find additional words beginning with *gl* in print in the room. Read the words together to confirm that the /gl/ sound begins each word.

Glasses (Who Needs 'em?)
by Lane Smith (Viking Penguin, 1991)
A young boy's doctor becomes increasingly
agitated as he tries to convince him that it's
not so bad to wear glasses. Readers will
enjoy the doctor's bizarre list of eyeglass
wearers.

ALA Notable Children's Books 1992.

Exploring Letter/Sound Relationships

Explore Together

Ⓐ • Buddy-read the *gl* book with a partner, identifying words that begin with /gl/*gl*.
• **Build-a-Word** • Provide cards with blend *gl* along with letter cards *a, e, o, u, d, w, v, b* to build and read words *glad, glue, glow, glove, globe*. List the words and read together.
• Invite children to use a word in a sentence to tell about themselves.
• Recite the rhymes on right with children to reinforce the /gl/ sound. Encourage children to write their own rhymes and poems.
Ⓐ • **Giant blend banner** • Write large letters *gl* on chart paper for children to draw and write words that begin with the blend *gl*. Display the banner and use as a resource for writing.

Explore on Your Own

🅰 • Provide blank glove-shape books for children to draw and write words with initial blend /gl/*gl*. Tell children to use the Build-a-Word chart and blend banner to think of words to write in their books.

glow   glue

Poems, Rhymes, and Jingles

Gloria's glittery glasses glisten.

Glossy gliders glimmer as they go.

*Glass covers windows to keep the winds away.
Gloves cover fingers to warm on a cold day.*

Using Ⓟ🅼 Books Together

Alphabet Blends and Digraphs *gr* Focus on words that have a blend with /g/ in the initial position. Make a game using words with initial blends *gl* and *gr*.

Out in the weather
(Starters Two)
Add sentences to tell about weather that can be described as gloomy or glorious.

Using the *Blends and Digraphs* Activity Masters

Mix and Match *and* Mixed-Up Letters
For additional practice with /gl/*gl*, engage children in the **manipulative** activities on pages 10 and 11.

Games and Puzzlers
To reinforce any letter/sound relationship, invite children to select one of the **interactive** ideas on pages 29–32.

Ⓐ *performance assessment* opportunities

🅰 projects for *portfolios*

gr *as in grapes*

Tips for the
English Language Learner

Make three columns on the chalkboard with heads *g, r, gr.* Write known words under each heading: *gate, goats, ring, rope, grapes, grass.* [See *Alphabet Starters g, r.*] Give each child letter cards for *g* and *r.* Say words that begin with *g, r,* and *gr.* The child holds up one or both letter cards to show the beginning letter(s). Write the word in the column. Read the words and underline the letter(s) that represents the initial sound.

Developing Phonemic Awareness

Read the Rhyme
• Read the rhyme "Grandma grows grapes," emphasizing the sound of the blend *gr* in the initial positions.
• Chant words *Grandma grows great green grapes.* Discuss how the words are alike.

Find the Sound
• Show how the /gr/ sound is made in the mouth.
(A) • Find something in the room whose name begins with /gr/ like *grandma's green grapes.* Provide clues such as: change the /m/ in *made* to /gr/ and what do you have? (*grade*); change the /s/ in *seen* to /gr/ and what do you have? (*green*); change the /s/ in *say* to /gr/ and what do you have? (*gray*)

Developing Print Awareness

Identify the Blend
• Write *green grapes* on the chalkboard and ask children to identify the letters that stand for the beginning sound. Confirm that letters *gr* stand for the sound /gr/.
• Reread the rhyme "Grandma grows grapes" and have children name the words they see that begin with the *gr* blend. Ask how *grapes* grow.

Find the Blend
• **In the book** • Make the sound /gr/ as the letters *gr* are traced on page 1 of the book. Read the book together, looking at pictures and reinforcing /gr/ as you read the words.
(A) • **Share a rhyme** • Volunteers can hold up the picture in the book as its name is said in the rhyme. Use the rhyme to focus on words that begin with the blend *gr.*

> *Who do we like to visit?*
> Grandmother *and* grandfather.
> *What do we like to eat?*
> Grapes *that are sweet.*
> *What is the color of* grass?
> Green, *I have seen.*
> *And the color of clouds full of rain?*
> Gray, *I explain.*

• Copy the rhyme onto chart paper. Read the rhyme together and underline words that begin with *gr.* Ask children to match each *gr* word in the rhyme with that in the book.
• Find additional words beginning with *gr* in print in the room. Read the words together to confirm that the /gr/ sound begins each word.

BOOKS
from your library shelf

The Grizzly Bear Family Book
by Michio Hoshino (North-South, 1994)
Grizzly bears will seem less frightening after seeing these beautiful photos taken of Alaska. Children's Choice.

Night in the Dinosaur Graveyard
by A. J. Wood (HarperCollins, 1994)
Lucy, Max, and Grandfather uncover ten dinosaur holograms as they spend a night in a graveyard.

Grandma Gets Grumpy
by Mary Hoffman (Dial Books, 1988)
When her five grandchildren take things too far, grandma gets grumpy! Children's Choice.

Exploring Letter/Sound Relationships

Explore Together

(A) • Buddy-read the *gr* book with a partner, identifying words that begin with /gr/*gr*.
• **Mixed-up letters** • Give each child a word with mixed-up letters to rearrange to form a word that begins with *gr*. Write the words on the chalkboard for the group to read. Mix up letters in words *grade, grape, gray, great, grin, grow, growl, ground, green, grass*.
• Recite the rhymes on right with children to reinforce the /gr/ sound. Encourage children to write their own rhymes and poems.

(A) • **Giant blend banner** • Write large letters *gr* on chart paper for children to draw and write words that begin with the blend *gr*. Display the banner and use as a resource for writing.

Explore on Your Own

(A) • Provide circles cut from green or purple construction paper. Children can write and illustrate a *gr* word on each circle and glue the circles onto paper to form a grape cluster. Children can make as many grapes for their clusters as they wish.

Poems, Rhymes, and Jingles

Gregory's grandparents grow great green grapes.

Grouchy green grasshoppers grumble in the grass.

*Gregory Griggs, Gregory Griggs,
Had twenty-seven grand wigs.
He wore them up, he wore them down,
To please the grown-ups of the town.
He wore them east, he wore them west,
But he never could tell which he loved the best.*

Using PM Books Together

Alphabet Blends and Digraphs br, cr, dr, fr, pr, tr Focus on words that have a variety of -*r* blends in the initial position.

Fishing (*Starters Two*) Gran is the heroine in this fishing story.

Using the *Blends and Digraphs* Activity Masters

Hidden Pictures *and* Pretty Presents
For additional practice with /gr/*gr*, engage children in the **manipulative** activities on pages 7 and 8.

Games and Puzzlers
To reinforce any letter/sound relationship, invite children to select one of the **interactive** ideas on pages 29–32.

 performance assessment opportunities

 projects for *portfolios*

Blends and Digraphs **25**

kn *as in knee*

Tips for the English Language Learner

Identify variant spellings for the sound /n/. Make word cards *nose, necklace, net, nails, needles, nest, nine [Alphabet Starters n]; knee, knob, knife, knitting, knot.* Say each word as children repeat the initial sound. Ask how the words are alike. Then display the cards and repeat the words for identification. Children can group the words according to beginning letter. Confirm that letters *n* and *kn* both stand for the /n/ sound.

Developing Phonemic Awareness

Read the Rhyme
- Read the rhyme "A rule to know," emphasizing the sound of the digraph *kn* in the initial positions.
- Chant words *know, knocking, knuckles, kneeling, knees.* Discuss how the words are alike.

Find the Sound
- Show how the /n/ sound is made in the mouth.
- **(A)** Find something in the room whose name begins with /n/ like *kneeling knees.* [Note: children may suggest words whose /n/ sound is spelled *n*. Provide clues such as: something I use to open the door (*knob*); the part of the leg you use to kneel (*knees*)].

Developing Print Awareness

Identify the Digraph
- Write *knees, knuckles* on the chalkboard and ask children to identify the letters that stand for the beginning sound. Confirm that letters *kn* stand for the sound /n/. Ask what other letter stands for the same sound. (*n*)
- Reread the rhyme "A rule to know" and have children name the words they see that begin with the *kn* blend.

Find the Digraph
- **In the book** • Make the sound /n/ as the letters *kn* are traced on page 1 of the book. Read the book together, looking at pictures and emphasizing /n/ as you read the words.
- **(A)** **Share a rhyme** • Volunteers can hold up the picture in the book as its name is said in the rhyme. Use the rhyme to focus on words that begin with the digraph *kn*.

> Kn *is for* knob *to turn,*
> knife *to cut,*
> knot *to tie,*
> knitting *to sew,*
> *and* knee…*I* know…*to* kneel.

- Copy the rhyme onto chart paper. Read the rhyme together and underline words that begin with *kn*. Ask children to match each *kn* word in the rhyme with that in the book.
- Find additional words beginning with *kn* in print in the room. Read the words together to confirm that the /n/ sound begins each word.

BOOKS
from your library shelf

I Know an Old Lady Who Swallowed a Fly
illustrated by Glen Rounds
(Holiday House, 1990)
Children will enjoy chiming in to recite this cumulative rhyme.

The Knight Who Was Afraid of the Dark
by Barbara Shook Hazen (Dial, 1989)
Sir Fred is a bold and brave knight, until he must face the dark.

You Know Who
by John Ciardi (Boyds Mills, 1991)
A "knock Knock" joke and other riddles for classmates to guess.

Exploring Letter/Sound Relationships

Explore Together

Ⓐ • Buddy-read the *kn* book with a partner, identifying words that begin with /n/*kn*.
• **Build-a-Word** • Provide cards with digraph *kn* along with letter cards *e, o, i, w, t, f, b, c, k* to build and read words *knew, knit, knife, knob, knock, knot, know*. List the words and read together.
• Recite the rhymes on right with children to reinforce the /n/ sound. Encourage children to write their own rhymes and poems.
Ⓐ • **Giant digraph banner** • Write large letters *kn* on chart paper for children to draw and write words that begin with the digraph *kn*. Display the banner and use as a resource for writing.

Explore on Your Own

Ⓐ • Provide blank books for children to draw and write words with initial digraph *kn*. Tell children to use the Build-a-Word chart and digraph banner to think of words to write in their books.

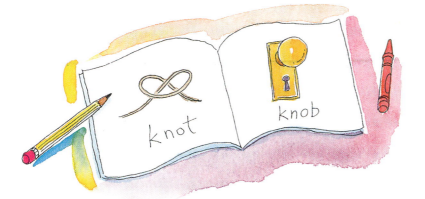

Poems, Rhymes, and Jingles

Ninety knights knew they needed new knapsacks.

*Knock on the door,
Peek in,
Turn the knob,
And walk in.*

*Knock, knock!
Who's there?
Ida.
Ida who?
Ida called first but I didn't know your number.*

Using **PM** Books Together

Alphabet Starters *n* List and compare words that begin with the same sound but have variant spellings.

Using the *Blends and Digraphs* Activity Masters

Picture Path *and* Digraph Dominoes
For additional practice with /n/*kn*, engage children in the **manipulative** activities on pages 20 and 22–23.

Games and Puzzlers
To reinforce any letter/sound relationship, invite children to select one of the **interactive** ideas on pages 29–32.

Ⓐ *performance assessment* opportunities

 projects for *portfolios*

ph as in phone

Identify variant spellings for the sound /f/. Make word cards *fish, fingers, fork, fire, feather, fence, five* [*Alphabet Starters f*]; *pheasant, photo, phone, photographer, photocopier.* Say each word as children repeat the initial sound. Ask how the words are alike. Then display the cards and repeat the words for identification. Children can group the words according to beginning letter. Confirm that letters *f* and *ph* both stand for the /f/ sound.

Developing Phonemic Awareness

Read the Rhyme
- Read the rhyme "Philip sees a pheasant," emphasizing the sound of the digraph *ph* in the initial positions.
- Chant words *Philip, pheasant, phone, photo*. Discuss how the words are alike.

Find the Sound
- Show how the /f/ sound is made in the mouth.
- **(A)** Find something in the room whose name begins with /f/ like *pheasant*. Note that children may suggest words that begin with the /f/*f* correspondence. Provide clues such as: the picture of our class taken by a camera (*photo*); something we use to call a friend or family member long distance (*phone*).

Developing Print Awareness

Identify the Digraph
- Write *phone* on the chalkboard and ask children to identify the letters that stand for the beginning sound. Confirm that letters *ph* stand for the sound /f/.
- Reread the rhyme "Philip sees a pheasant" and have children name the words they see that begin with the *ph* digraph.

Find the Digraph
- **In the book** • Make the sound /f/ as the letters *ph* are traced on page 1 of the book. Read the book together, looking at pictures and emphasizing /f/ as you read the words.
- **(A)** • **Share a rhyme** • Volunteers can hold up the picture in the book as its name is said in the rhyme. Use the rhyme to focus on words that begin with the digraph *ph*.

> A pheasant *is a bird you know*
> *with brightly colored feathers, so*
> *to get a* photo *shot of her*
> photographers *must flock to her.*
> *It might be so much easier*
> *to print pictures on a* photocopier,
> *but should you see a* pheasant *pass,*
> *get on the* phone *and call me fast!*

- Copy the rhyme onto chart paper. Read the rhyme together and underline words that begin with *ph*. Ask children to match each *ph* word in the rhyme with that in the book.
- Find additional words beginning with *ph* in print in the room. Read the words together to confirm that the /f/ sound begins each word.

BOOKS
from your library shelf

Phil the Ventriloquist
by Robert Kraus (Greenwillow, 1989)
Phil the rabbit seems to annoy his parents
with his ventriloquism, until the day when
he saves them all from a burglar.

Simple Pictures Are Best
by Nancy Willard (Harcourt Brace, 1977)
A photographer tells a couple that simple
pictures are best, but they continue to add
every animal and household thing they can
find to be in their photo.

Exploring Letter/Sound Relationships

Explore Together

(A) • Buddy-read the *ph* book with a partner, identifying words that begin with /f/*ph*.
• Recite the rhymes on right with children to reinforce the /f/ sound. Encourage
children to write their own rhymes and poems.
• ***Ph* crossword puzzle** • Write the word *photographer* on the board. Have
children write other words with *ph* by hooking onto letters in the word and
writing across or down to build a word puzzle.

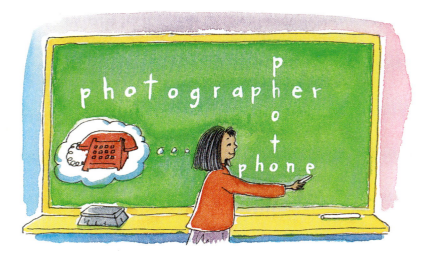

(A) • **Giant digraph banner** • Write large letters *ph* on chart paper for children to
draw and write words that begin with the digraph *ph*. Display the banner and
use as a resource for writing.

Explore on Your Own

(A) • Provide blank phone-shape books for children to draw and write words with
initial digraph *ph*. Tell children to use the Build-a-Word chart and digraph
banner to think of words to write in their books.

Using (PM) Books Together

Alphabet Starters *f*
Focus on words that have
variant spellings for the
/f/ sound.

Starters One collection
Choose any book and
tell the story using
the photos.

Using the *Blends and Digraphs* Activity Masters

**Picture Path *and*
Digraph Dominoes**
For additional practice with /f/*ph*,
engage children in the **manipulative**
activities on pages 20 and 22–23.

Games and Puzzlers
To reinforce any letter/sound relationship, invite children to select
one of the **interactive** ideas on
pages 29–32.

 performance assessment opportunities

 projects for *portfolios*

pl as in plane

Developing Phonemic Awareness

Read the Rhyme

• Read the rhyme "Plenty of plums," emphasizing the sound of the blend *pl* in the initial position.
• Chant words *plenty, plums, pleasant, plump.* Discuss how the words are alike.

Find the Sound

• Show how the /pl/ sound is made in the mouth.
Ⓐ • Find something in the room whose name begins with /pl/ like *plump plums.*
• Provide clues such as: something green growing in a pot (*plant*); a sign you use when you add two numbers (+ *or plus*).

Developing Print Awareness

Identify the Blend

• Write *plum* on the chalkboard and ask children to identify the letters that stand for the beginning sound. Confirm that letters *pl* stand for the sound /pl/.
• Reread the rhyme "Plenty of plums" and have children name the words they see that begin with the *pl* blend.

Find the Blend

• **In the book** • Make the sound /pl/ as the letters *pl* are traced on page 1 of the book. Read the book together, looking at pictures and emphasizing /pl/ as you read the words.
Ⓐ • **Share a rhyme** • Volunteers can hold up the picture in the book as its name is said in the rhyme. Use the rhyme to focus on words that begin with the blend *pl*.

> The blend pl *is all around;*
> *The first we see is in* playground.
> Pl *starts* plane *and if you add -ts,*
> Planets *is the word to guess.*
> *Change some letters or shuffle a few,*
> *And out comes* plates *and* plants *for you.*

• Copy the rhyme onto chart paper. Read the rhyme together and underline words that begin with *pl*. Ask children to match each *pl* word in the rhyme with that in the book.
• Find additional words beginning with *pl* in print in the room. Read the words together to confirm that the /pl/ sound begins each word.

BOOKS
from your library shelf

A Playhouse for Monster
by Virginia Mueller (Albert Whitman, 1985)
Monster puts a "Keep Out" sign on his playhouse, but has a problem when a friend arrives.

Bringing the Rain to Kapiti Plain
by Verna Aardema (Dial, 1981)
A retelling of a cumulative Kenya tale about the animals in a drought. A good review of long *a* words.

Thump and Plunk
by Janice May Udry (Harper & Row, 1981)
Children may enjoy creating an unusual *Pl* name for themselves like the character in the story. Story words provide a good review of short *u* as well.

Exploring Letter/Sound Relationships

Explore Together

Ⓐ • Buddy-read the *pl* book with a partner, identifying words that begin with /pl/*pl*.
• **Build-a-Word** • Provide cards with blend *pl* along with letter cards *a, e, u, c, n, t, s, m* to build and read words *place, plane, plan, plant, planet, plate, please, plum, plus*. List the words and read together.

• Recite the rhymes on right with children to reinforce the /pl/ sound. Encourage children to write their own rhymes and poems.
Ⓐ • **Giant blend banner** • Write large letters *pl* on chart paper for children to draw and write words that begin with the blend *pl*. Display the banner and use as a resource for writing.

Explore on Your Own

Ⓐ • Provide blank round-shape books with paper plate covers for children to draw and write words with initial blend *pl*. Tell children to use the Build-a-Word chart and blend banner to think of words to write in their books.

Using the *Blends and Digraphs* Activity Masters

Mix and Match *and* Mixed-Up Letters
For additional practice with /pl/*pl*, engage children in the **manipulative** activities on pages 10 and 11.

Games and Puzzlers
To reinforce any letter/sound relationship, invite children to select one of the **interactive** ideas on pages 29–32.

Using Ⓟⓜ Books Together

Alphabet Blends and Digraphs *bl, cl, fl, gl, sl*
Focus on words that have a variety of *-l* blends in the initial position.

Playing (*Starters One*)
Reread the story. Then use words such as *play, playground, playmates* to talk about and to write a plan for games to play outside.

Ⓐ *performance assessment* opportunities

Ⓐ projects for *portfolios*

pr *as in prince*

Developing Phonemic Awareness

Read the Rhyme

- Read the rhyme "My dog Prince wins prizes," emphasizing the sound of the blend *pr* in the initial positions.
- Chant words *Prince, prizes, prancing, proud, pricks, praise, proper*. Discuss how the words are alike.

Find the Sound

- Show how the /pr/ sound is made in the mouth.
- (A) • Find something in the room whose name begins with /pr/ like *Prince*. Provide clues such as: when you write letters on paper you…(*print*); if you win a contest you might receive a…(*prize*).

Developing Print Awareness

Identify the Blend

- Write *prince* on the chalkboard and ask children to identify the letters that stand for the beginning sound. Confirm that letters *pr* stand for the sound /pr/.
- Reread the rhyme "My dog Prince wins prizes" and have children name the words they see that begin with the *pr* blend.

Find the Blend

- **In the book** • Make the sound /pr/ as the letters *pr* are traced on page 1 in the book. Read the book together, looking at pictures and reinforcing /pr/ as you read the words.
- (A) • **Share a rhyme** • Volunteers can hold up the picture in the book as its name is said in the rhyme. Use the rhyme to focus on words that begin with the blend *pr*.

> Printing *begins with* pr;
> propeller *does too.*
> *So does the word* present,
> *a nice gift just for you.*
> *When you write* prize,
> *what letters start the word?*
> *Two more are* prince *and* princess;
> pr *starts them—have you heard?*

- Copy the rhyme onto chart paper. Read the rhyme together and underline words that begin with *pr*. Ask children to match each *pr* word in the rhyme with that in the book.
- Find additional words beginning with *pr* in print in the room. Read the words together to confirm that the /pr/ sound begins each word.

Exploring Letter/Sound Relationships

Explore Together

(A) • Buddy-read the *pr* book with a partner, identifying words that begin with /pr/*pr*.
• **Finish-a-Word**. • Write words on the chalkboard: __etty, __ice, __int, __etzel, __esent, __ize, __une, __ince. Write *pr* to finish the words and read together. Children can choose a word to write with scrambled letters on paper and ask a partner to rewrite and read.

• Recite the rhymes on right with children to reinforce the /pr/ sound. Encourage children to write their own rhymes and poems.
(A) • **Giant blend banner** • Write large letters *pr* on chart paper for children to draw and write words that begin with the blend *pr*. Display the banner and use as a resource for writing.

Explore on Your Own

(A) • Provide blank books for children to draw and write words with initial blend /pr/*pr*. Children can decorate the book cover to resemble a wrapped present. Tell children to use the blend banner to think of words to write in their books.

Poems, Rhymes, and Jingles

Prickly pears prick when you pick.

Presents and prizes are pleasant surprises.

Mary had a pretty bird,
Feathers bright and yellow.
She named her songbird
Prince, of course.
He was a pretty fellow.

Using (PM) Books Together

Alphabet Blends and Digraphs *spr* Compare initial sounds in words when *s-* is added to the blend *pr*.

Using the *Blends and Digraphs* Activity Masters

Story Time *and* Pretty Presents
For additional practice with /pr/*pr*, engage children in the **manipulative** activities on pages 6 and 8.

Games and Puzzlers
To reinforce any letter/sound relationship, invite children to select one of the **interactive** ideas on pages 29–32.

 performance assessment opportunities

 projects for *portfolios*

SC as in scarf

Make three columns on the chalkboard with heads *s, c, sc*. Write known words under each heading: *sun, socks; cat, cake; scale, scarf.* [See *Alphabet Starters c, s.*] Give each child letter cards for *s* and *c*. Say words that begin with *s, c,* or *sc*. The child holds up one or both letter cards to show the beginning letter(s). Write the word in the column. Read the words and underline the letter(s) that represents the initial sound.

Developing Phonemic Awareness

Read the Rhyme
- Read the rhyme "Hurry-scurry," emphasizing the sound of the blend *sc* in the initial positions.
- Chant words *scurry, scamper, scuttle.* Discuss how the words are alike.

Find the Sound
- Show how the /sk/ sound is made in the mouth.
- (A) Find something in the room whose name begins with /sk/ like *scurry*. Some children may suggest words with /sk/ spelled *sk*. Provide clues such as: something we use in the math center to weigh things (*scale*); a cloth worn on the head or around the neck (*scarf*).

Developing Print Awareness

Identify the Blend
- Write *scurry* on the chalkboard and ask children to identify the letters that stand for the beginning sound. Confirm that letters *sc* stand for the sound /sk/.
- Reread the rhyme "Hurry-scurry" and have children name the words they see that begin with the *sc* blend. Children can demonstrate how to *scurry, scuttle,* and *scamper.*

Find the Blend
- **In the book** • Make the sound /sk/ as the letters *sc* are traced on page 1 of the book. Read the book together, looking at pictures and reinforcing /sk/ as you read the words.
- (A) • **Share a rhyme** • Volunteers can hold up the picture in the book as its name is said in the rhyme. Use the rhyme to focus on words that begin with the blend *sc*.

> Scaffolding *has great height;*
> Scorpion *is a frightful sight.*
> Scales *show how much things weigh;*
> Scarf *is warm on a wintry day;*
> Scarecrow *frightens the birds away.*

- Copy the rhyme onto chart paper. Read the rhyme together and underline words that begin with *sc*. Ask children to match each *sc* word in the rhyme with that in the book.
- Find additional words beginning with *sc* in print in the room. Read the words together to confirm that the /sk/ sound begins each word.

BOOKS
from your library shelf

The Scary Book
compiled by Joanna Cole and Stephanie Calmenson (Morrow, 1991)
This collection of stories, poems, tricks, riddles, and jokes will thrill any child who likes a scary theme.

Pack 109
by Mike Thaler (Harper & Row, 1986)
Children will chuckle as a pack of scouts tries to earn their merit badges in this five-chapter book.

Sam the Scarecrow
by Sharon Gordon (Troll, 1980)
Children may want to try creating a scarecrow of their own after reading about Sam.

Exploring Letter/Sound Relationships

Explore Together

Ⓐ • Buddy-read the *sc* book with a partner, identifying words that begin with /sk/*sc*.
• *Sc scramble* • Draw two score boxes on the chalkboard, one for each team you form. Players on each team work together to rearrange letters written on the chalkboard or on cards to form a word that begins with *sc*. Players score a point for each correct word. Use words: *scat, scout, scare, scarf, scar, scale, scoop, score, scarecrow*.
• Recite the rhymes on right with children to reinforce the /sk/ sound. Encourage children to write their own rhymes and poems.
Ⓐ • **Giant blend banner** • Write large letters *sc* on chart paper with the outline shape of a scarecrow for children to draw and write words that begin with the blend *sc*. Display the banner and use as a resource for writing.

Explore on Your Own

Ⓐ • Provide blank scarf-shape books for children to draw and write words with initial blend /sk/*sc*. Tell children to use the blend banner to think of words to write in their books.

Poems, Rhymes, and Jingles

Scowling scarecrow scares scores of crows.

Scorpions scuttle across scorching sand.

*Scarecrow, scarecrow,
I'm glad you're here.
Scare the crows, so they
won't come near.
Guard the seed scattered
in the field,
So a corn crop it will yield.
Scat, birds, scat, you
cannot eat!
The scarecrow waves his
arms and feet.*

Using **PM** Books Together

Alphabet Blends and Digraphs *sk* Focus on words that have variant spellings for the initial sound /sk/.

Dressing up
(Starters One)
Have children suggest other costumes that are "scary."

Using the *Blends and Digraphs* Activity Masters

Shoo, Crow!, Missing Blends, *and* Scoreboard
For additional practice with /sk/*sc*, engage children in the **manipulative** activities on pages 12, 14, and 27.

Games and Puzzlers
To reinforce any letter/sound relationship, invite children to select one of the **interactive** ideas on pages 29–32.

Ⓐ *performance assessment* opportunities

Ⓐ projects for *portfolios*

scr as in scrubbing brush

Tips for the
English Language Learner

Make three columns on the chalkboard with heads *s, sc, scr.* Write known words under each heading: *socks, seven, scarecrow, scarf, scribble, screen.* [See *Alphabet Starters s* and *Alphabet Blends and Digraphs sc* for words.] Give each child letter cards for *s, c, r.* Say words that begin with *s, sc, scr.* The child holds up one, two, or all three letter cards to show the beginning letter(s). Write the word in the column. Read the words and underline the letter(s) that represents the initial sound.

Developing Phonemic Awareness

Read the Rhyme
- Read the rhyme "Scrubbing the wall," emphasizing the sound of the blend *scr* in the initial positions.
- Chant words *scrubbing, scrawl, scribbles, scratches.* Discuss how the words are alike.

Find the Sound
- Show how the /skr/ sound is made in the mouth.
- (A) Find something in the room whose name begins with /skr/ like *scrubbing.* Provide clues such as: something we use to watch a movie (*screen*); something we use to keep photos of our class trips (*scrapbook*).

Developing Print Awareness

Identify the Blend
- Write *scrubbing* on the chalkboard and ask children to identify the letters that stand for the beginning sound. Confirm that letters *scr* stand for the sound /skr/.
- Reread the rhyme "Scrubbing the wall" and have children name the words they see that begin with the *scr* blend. Make scrubbing motions while reading.

Find the Blend
- **In the book** • Make the sound /skr/ as the letters *scr* are traced on page 1 in the book. Read the book together, looking at pictures and reinforcing /skr/ as you read the words.
- (A) **Share a rhyme** • Volunteers can hold up the picture in the book as its name is said in the rhyme. Use the rhyme to focus on words that begin with the blend *scr.*

> Scr *is for* screen *and a* scratch *from my cat,*
> *For* screws *to hold the hinges on each and every door,*
> *And* scrubbing *brush to clean the* scribbles
> *From the walls and floor.*

- Copy the rhyme onto chart paper. Read the rhyme together and underline words that begin with *scr.* Ask children to match each *scr* word in the rhyme with that in the book.
- Find additional words beginning with *scr* in print in the room. Read the words together to confirm that the /skr/ sound begins each word.

Exploring Letter/Sound Relationships

Explore Together

(A) • Buddy-read the *scr* book with a partner, identifying words that begin with /skr/*scr.*
• **Build-a-Word** • Provide cards with blend *scr* along with letter cards *a, e, u, b, w, m, p* to build and read words *scrub, screw, scream, scrap, scrape*. List the words and read together.

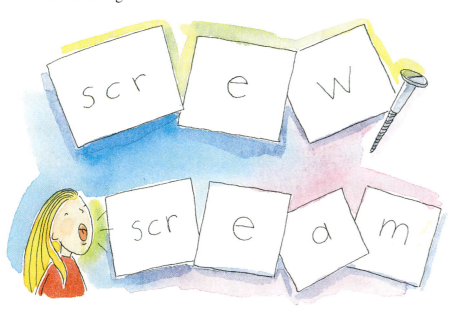

• Recite the rhymes on right with children to reinforce the /skr/ sound. Encourage children to write their own rhymes and poems.
(A) • **Giant blend banner** • Write large letters *scr* on chart paper for children to draw and write words that begin with the blend *scr.* Display the banner and use as a resource for writing.

Explore on Your Own

(A) • Provide blank books for children to draw and write words with initial blend /skr/*scr.* Tell children to use the Build-a-Word chart and blend banner to think of words to write in their books.

Using the *Blends and Digraphs* Activity Masters

Building Blocks *and* Scoreboard
For additional practice with /skr/*scr,* engage children in the **manipulative** activities on pages 24 and 27.

Games and Puzzlers
To reinforce any letter/sound relationship, invite children to select one of the **interactive** ideas on pages 29–32.

  performance assessment opportunities

  projects for *portfolios*

Poems, Rhymes, and Jingles

Scrub the scribbles and scrap the scratches.

*SCRITCH SCRATCH!
What is that?
SCRUNCH MUNCH!
I have a hunch.
Cat's in the scraps,
looking for lunch!*

Using **PM** Books Together

Alphabet Blends and Digraphs *spr, str, thr*
Focus on words that have three-letter blends with -*r.*

A house (*Starters One*)
What are some things around the house that need scrubbing?

sh *as in shoes*

Tips for the English Language Learner

Make three columns on the chalkboard with heads *s, h, sh*. Write known words under each heading: *sun, socks, hats, hand, shoes, ship*. [See *Alphabet Starters s, h.*] Give each child letter cards for *s* and *h*. Say words that begin with *s, h,* or *sh*. The child holds up one or both letter cards to show the beginning letter(s). Write the word in the column. Read the words and underline the letter(s) that represents the initial sound.

Developing Phonemic Awareness

Read the Rhyme

• Read the rhyme "The shy shellfish," emphasizing the sound of the digraph *sh* in the initial and final positions.
• Chant words *shy, shellfish, shiny, shell, shuts*. Discuss how the words are alike.

Find the Sound

• Show how the /sh/ sound is made in the mouth.
Ⓐ • Find something in the room whose name begins with /sh/ like *shy shellfish*.
• Provide clues such as: something on your feet (*shoes*); something with sleeves and buttons (*shirt*); something to hold books (*shelf*).

Developing Print Awareness

Identify the Digraph

• Write *shy shellfish* on the chalkboard and ask children to identify the letters that stand for the beginning sound. Confirm that letters *sh* stand for the sound /sh/.
• Reread the rhyme "The shy shellfish" and have children name the words they see that begin with the *sh* digraph.

Find the Digraph

• **In the book** • Make the sound /sh/ as the letters *sh* are traced on page 1 of the book. Read the book together, looking at pictures and emphasizing /sh/ as you read the words.
Ⓐ • **Share a rhyme** • Volunteers can hold up the picture in the book as its name is said in the rhyme. Use the rhyme to focus on words that begin with the digraph *sh*.

Sh is for shovel and shoes and sharks in oceans deep; for ships that sail the blue sea and for the farmer's sheep.

• Copy the rhyme onto chart paper. Read the rhyme together and underline words that begin with *sh*. Ask children to match each *sh* word in the rhyme with that in the book.
• Find additional words beginning with *sh* in print in the room. Read the words together to confirm that the /sh/ sound begins each word.

BOOKS
from your library shelf

Sheep in a Shop
by Nancy Shaw (Houghton Mifflin, 1991)
This is a rollicking shopping trip with five sheep who need a gift for a friend.

Sheep in a Ship
by Nancy Shaw (Houghton Mifflin, 1989)
In this sheep tale, the rhymed text tells about the sheep as pirates on a deep-sea trip.

Shhh!
by Sally Grindley (Little, Brown, 1992)
Two tiny creatures go on a tiptoe journey through a giant's castle

Exploring Letter/Sound Relationships

Explore Together

(A) • Buddy-read the *sh* book with a partner, identifying words that begin with /sh/*sh*.
- **Build-a-Word** • Provide cards with digraph *sh* along with letter cards *a, o, e, i, p, k, r, t* to build and read words *shop, shake, shape, share, shark, sharp, she, ship, shoe, shore, short, shot.* List the words and read together. Use as a resource for tongue twisters.
- Recite the rhymes on right with children to reinforce the /sh/ sound. Encourage children to write their own rhymes and poems.

(A) • **Giant digraph banner** • Write large letters *sh* on chart paper for children to draw and write words that begin with the digraph *sh*. Display the banner and use as a resource for writing. You may want to include words that end with *sh* as well.

Explore on Your Own

(A) • Provide blank shoe-shape books for children to draw and write words with initial digraph *sh*. Tell children to use the Build-a-Word chart and digraph banner to think of words to write in their books.

ship   shoe

Using the *Blends and Digraphs* Activity Masters

Across and Down, Lunch Shack, and Digraph Dominoes
For additional practice with /sh/*sh*, engage children in the **manipulative** activities on pages 16, 18, and 22–23.

Games and Puzzlers
To reinforce any letter/sound relationship, invite children to select one of the **interactive** ideas on pages 29–32.

Using (PM) Books Together

Alphabet Blends and Digraphs *ch, ph, th, wh*
Focus on words with -*h* digraphs.

The shopping mall
(Starters One)
Reinforce words with *sh* and *st*.

The rock pools
(Starters Two)
Children get a look at shellfish in their natural habitat.

 performance assessment opportunities

 projects for *portfolios*

sk as in skiing

Make three columns on the chalkboard with heads *s, k, sk*. Write known words under each heading: *saw, seven, keys, kitten, ski, sky*. [See *Alphabet Starters s, k*.] Give each child letter cards for *s* and *k*. Say words that begin with *s, k,* and *sk*. The child holds up one or both letter cards to show the beginning letter(s). Write the word in the column. Read the words and underline the letter(s) that represents the initial sound.

Developing Phonemic Awareness

Read the Rhyme

- Read the "Skipping rhyme," emphasizing the sound of the blend *sk* in the initial positions.
- Chant words *skipping, skate, skates, skid, ski, skip*. Discuss how the words are alike.

Find the Sound

- Show how the /sk/ sound is made in the mouth.
- Find something in the room whose name begins with /sk/ like *skip*. Provide clues such as: what covers your body? (*skin*); what do you see out the window? (*sky*)

Developing Print Awareness

Identify the Blend

- Write *skipping* on the chalkboard and ask children to identify the letters that stand for the beginning sound. Confirm that letters *sk* stand for the sound /sk/.
- Reread the "Skipping rhyme" and have children name the words they see that begin with the *sk* blend.

Find the Blend

- **In the book** • Make the sound /sk/ as the letters *sk* are traced on page 1 of the book. Read the book together, looking at pictures and emphasizing /sk/ as you read the words.
- **Share a rhyme** • Volunteers can hold up the picture in the book as its name is said in the rhyme. Use the rhyme to focus on words that begin with the blend *sk*.

  > Sk *is for* skateboard
  > *for* skirt *and for* ski;
  > *the* sky *up above*
  > *and the* skeleton *inside me.*

- Copy the rhyme onto chart paper. Read the rhyme together and underline words that begin with *sk*. Ask children to match each *sk* word in the rhyme with that in the book.
- Find additional words beginning with *sk* in print in the room. Read the words together to confirm that the /sk/ sound begins each word.

BOOKS
from your library shelf

A Book About Your Skeleton
by Ruth Belov Gross (Scholastic, 1994)
Whimsical illustrations and humorous text make learning about your skeleton fun.

Skip to My Lou
by Nadine Bernard Westcott
(Little, Brown, 1989)
In this new "Skip to my Lou" the farm animals create a hullabaloo while the farmer is away.

Skyfire
by Frank Asch (Prentice Hall, 1984)
A fire in the sky turns out to be a brilliant rainbow.

Exploring Letter/Sound Relationships

Explore Together
A • Buddy-read the *sk* book with a partner, identifying words that begin with /sk/*sk*.

• **Build-a-Word** • Provide cards with blend *sk* along with letter cards *i, p, n, d, m, r, t* to build and read words *ski, skip, skin, skid, skim, skirt.* List the words and read together.
• Recite the rhymes on right with children to reinforce the /sk/ sound. Encourage children to write their own rhymes and poems.
A • **Giant blend banner** • Write large letters *sk* on chart paper for children to draw and write words that begin with the blend *sk.* Display the banner and use as a resource for writing.

Explore on Your Own
A • Provide blank books with covers the color of the sky for children to draw and write words with initial blend /sk/*sk*. Tell children to use the Build-a-Word chart and blend banner to think of words to write in their books.

Using the *Blends and Digraphs* Activity Masters

Picture Clue Puzzle *and* Missing Blends
For additional practice with /sk/*sk*, engage children in the **manipulative** activities on pages 13 and 14.

Games and Puzzlers
To reinforce any letter/sound relationship, invite children to select one of the **interactive** ideas on pages 29–32.

Using **PM** Books Together

Alphabet Blends and Digraphs *sc* Focus on words that have the same initial sound but different spellings.

My accident
(Starters Two)
A boy has an accident with a skateboard.

 performance assessment opportunities

 projects for *portfolios*

sl *as in slide*

Tips for the English Language Learner

Make three columns on the chalkboard with heads *s, l, sl*. Write known words under each heading: *seven, sun, leaf, ladder, sled, sleeve*. [See *Alphabet Starters s, l* .] Give each child letter cards for *s* and *l*. Say words that begin with *s, l,* or *sl*. The child holds up one or both letter cards to show the beginning letter(s). Write the word in the column. Read the words and underline the letter(s) that represents the initial sound.

Developing Phonemic Awareness

Read the Rhyme

- Read the rhyme "Slippery sled," emphasizing the sound of the blend *sl* in the initial positions.
- Chant words *slippery, sled, slow, slithering, sliding*. Discuss how the words are alike.

Find the Sound

- Show how the /sl/ sound is made in the mouth.
- Ⓐ • Find something in the room whose name begins with /sl/ like *slippery sled*. Provide clues such as: if you change /t/ in *tacks* to /sl/, what do you have? (*slacks*); if you change /d/ in *deep* to /sl/, what do you have? (*sleep*).

Developing Print Awareness

Identify the Blend

- Write *slippery sled* on the chalkboard and ask children to identify the letters that stand for the beginning sound. Confirm that letters *sl* stand for the sound /sl/.
- Reread the rhyme "Slippery sled" and have children name the words they see that begin with the *sl* blend.

Find the Blend

- **In the book** • Make the sound /sl/ as the letters *sl* are traced on page 1 in the book. Read the book together, looking at pictures and emphasizing /sl/ as you read the words.
- Ⓐ • **Share a rhyme** • Volunteers can hold up the picture in the book as its name is said in the rhyme. Use the rhyme to focus on words that begin with the blend *sl*.

> Sl *is on the go*
> *in a playground* slide
> *and a* sled *on the snow;*
> Sl *begins other words you meet—*
> *a* sleeve *on a shirt,*
> *a* sling *for an arm,*
> *and* slippers *for your feet.*

- Copy the rhyme onto chart paper. Read the rhyme together and underline words that begin with *sl*. Ask children to match each *sl* word in the rhyme with that in the book.
- Find additional words beginning with *sl* in print in the room. Read the words together to confirm that the /sl/ sound begins each word.

BOOKS
from your library shelf

Six Sleepy Sheep
by Jeffie Ross Gordon (Boyds Mills, 1991)
Six sleepy sheep slumber on soft pillows
until... [This is a fun story chock full of *s*
blend words.]

The Sleepytime Book
by Jan Wahl (Tambourine, 1992)
The rhythmic, alliterative text tells about
charming animals as they go about their
nighttime activities.

Arthur's First Sleepover
by Marc Brown (Little, Brown, 1994)
Arthur the Aardvark plans his first outside
sleepover with friends who didn't count on
an alien invasion!

Exploring Letter/Sound Relationships

Explore Together

A • Buddy-read the *sl* book with a partner, identifying words that begin with /sl/*sl*.
- **Be a sleuth** • Write words on the chalkboard: *slacks, slam, sled, sleep, sleeve, slim, slow, sloppy*. Volunteers trace *sl* in a word and read it. Give a clue to identify each word: to close with force; to move with little speed; pants; clothing that covers the arm; used to glide across snow; to rest at night; messy; thin.
- Recite the rhymes on right with children to reinforce the /sl/ sound. Encourage children to write their own rhymes and poems.

A • **Giant blend banner** • Write large letters *sl* on chart paper for children to draw and write words that begin with the blend *sl*. Display the banner and use as a resource for writing.

Explore on Your Own

A • Provide blank bunny slipper-shape books for children to draw and write words with initial blend *sl*. Tell children to use the blend banner to think of words to write in their books.

Poems, Rhymes, and Jingles

Slick's sled slipped on slippery slush.

The sleepy slow slouch slumbered.

Slippery Sam bought a sled, Went slipping and sliding and bumped his head, Felt quite sleepy and went to bed.

slide   sled

Using the *Blends and Digraphs* Activity Masters

Mix and Match *and* Mixed-Up Letters
For additional practice with /sl/*sl*, engage children in the **manipulative** activities on pages 10 and 11.

Games and Puzzlers
To reinforce any letter/sound relationship, invite children to select one of the **interactive** ideas on pages 29–32.

Using 🔴PM Books Together

Alphabet Blends and Digraphs *bl, cl, fl, gl, pl*
Focus on words that have a variety of *-l* blends in the initial position.

Fishing
(Starters Two)
Rewrite the book, using sledding in place of fishing.

 performance assessment opportunities

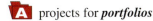 projects for *portfolios*

sm *as in smile*

Tips for the
English Language Learner

Write words on the chalkboard: *mile, woke, fog, sock, sell, wall.* Ask children to say each word and isolate the beginning sound. Then they can change the beginning sound to /sm/ to say a new word. Write the new word on the chalkboard.

Developing Phonemic Awareness

Read the Rhyme
- Read the rhyme "Smoke and flames," emphasizing the sound of the blend *sm* in the initial positions.
- Chant words *smoke, small, smell.* Discuss how the words are alike.

Find the Sound
- Show how the /sm/ sound is made in the mouth.
(A) - Find something in the room whose name begins with /sm/ like *smoke.* Provide clues such as: the opposite of *big* and starts with /sm/ (*small*); the opposite of *frown* and starts with /sm/ (*smile*).

Developing Print Awareness

Identify the Blend
- Write *smoke* on the chalkboard and ask children to identify the letters that stand for the beginning sound. Confirm that letters *sm* stand for the sound /sm/.
- Reread the rhyme "Smoke and flames" and have children name the words they see that begin with the *sm* blend.

Find the Blend
- **In the book** • Make the sound /sm/ as the letters *sm* are traced on page 1 in the book. Read the book together, looking at pictures and reinforcing /sm/ as you read the words.
(A) - **Share a rhyme** • Volunteers can hold up the picture in the book as its name is said in the rhyme. Use the rhyme to focus on words that begin with the blend *sm.*

> *Put* sm *with* -udge, *and you have…* smudge.
> *Put* sm *with* -ile, *and you have…* smile.
> *Put* sm *with* -ock, *and you have…* smock.
> *Put* sm *with* -oke, *and you have…* smoke *and* smoke detector.

- Copy the rhyme onto chart paper. Read the rhyme together and underline words that begin with *sm.* Ask children to match each *sm* word in the rhyme with that in the book.
- Find additional words beginning with *sm* in print in the room. Read the words together to confirm that the /sm/ sound begins each word.

The Smallest Cow in the World
by Katharine Paterson (HarperCollins, 1991)
When Marvin's father must sell the farm and his favorite cow, Rosie, the boy creates an imaginary tiny cow who does naughty things in the family.

Princess Smartypants
by Babette Cole (G. P. Putnam's, 1987)
Princess Smartypants lives up to her name when she devises difficult tasks for her would-be suitors.

Exploring Letter/Sound Relationships

Explore Together

Ⓐ • Buddy-read the *sm* book with a partner, identifying words that begin with /sm/*sm*.

• **Build-a-Word** • Provide cards with blend *sm* along with letter cards *a, e, i, o, l, l, k, g, c, y* to build and read words *smile, smoke, smoky, smog, smock, smell, small*. List the words and read together.

• Recite the rhymes on right with children to reinforce the /sm/ sound. Encourage children to write their own rhymes and poems.

Ⓐ • **Giant blend banner** • Write large letters *sm* on chart paper for children to draw and write words that begin with the blend *sm*. Display the banner and use as a resource for writing.

Explore on Your Own

Ⓐ • Provide blank round-shape books for children to draw and write words with initial blend /sm/*sm*. Children can make a smiling face cover. Tell children to use the Build-a-Word chart and blend banner to think of words to write in their books.

Poems, Rhymes, and Jingles

Smiley Small smelled smoke.

Smiling girls and smiling boys,
Come and buy my little toys;
Sweet-smelling bears
of gingerbread,
Small trucks and wagons
painted red.

Using Ⓟ Ⓜ Books Together

Alphabet Blends and Digraphs *sc, sl, sk, sn, sp, st, sw* Focus on words that have a variety of *s*-blends in the initial position.

Little things
(Starters One)
After reading, children can write sentences about small things they have.

Using the *Blends and Digraphs* Activity Masters

Picture Clue Puzzle *and* Missing Blends
For additional practice with /sm/*sm*, engage children in the **manipulative** activities on pages 13 and 14.

Games and Puzzlers
To reinforce any letter/sound relationship, invite children to select one of the **interactive** ideas on pages 29–32.

Ⓐ *performance assessment* opportunities

Ⓐ projects for *portfolios*

sn as in snake

Tips for the
English Language Learner

Focus on isolating the beginning sounds in words. Have children change the beginning sound in each of the following words to /sn/ and say the new word. Write the *sn* words as they are given. Use words: *lap (snap), rake (snake), nail (snail), sack (snack),weak (sneak), cliff (sniff), lip (snip), more (snore), low (snow).* Read the *sn* words together.

Developing Phonemic Awareness

Read the Rhyme
- Read the rhyme "Snoozing and snoring," emphasizing the sound of the blend *sn* in the initial positions.
- Chant words *snoozing, snoring, snoozes, snores, snort.* Discuss how the words are alike.

Find the Sound
- Show how the /sn/ sound is made in the mouth.
- Ⓐ Find something in the room whose name begins with /sn/ like *snores.* Provide clues such as: something you wear on your feet (*sneakers*); something you have in your lunchbox (*snack*).

Developing Print Awareness

Identify the Blend
- Write *snoozing* on the chalkboard and ask children to identify the letters that stand for the beginning sound. Confirm that letters *sn* stand for the sound /sn/.
- Reread the rhyme "Snoozing and snoring" and have children name the words they see that begin with the *sn* blend. As you reread together, invite some children to provide snoring sound effects.

Find the Blend
- **In the book** • Make the sound /sn/ as the letters *sn* are traced on page 1 of the book. Read the book together, looking at pictures and emphasizing /sn/ as you read the words.
- Ⓐ **Share a rhyme** • Volunteers can hold up the picture in the book as its name is said in the rhyme. Use the rhyme to focus on words that begin with the blend *sn.*

> Sn *words are everywhere you go.*
> *Hear* sn *in* sneeze. *See* sn *in* snow.
> *There goes* sn *in a slow-moving* snail.
> *Again in a* snake *without legs or tail.*
> *You can build an* sn *word—yes, you can!*
> *When you make your very own* sn*—snowman!*

- Copy the rhyme onto chart paper. Read the rhyme together and underline words that begin with *sn.* Ask children to match each *sn* word in the rhyme with that in the book.
- Find additional words beginning with *sn* in print in the room. Read the words together to confirm that the /sn/ sound begins each word.

BOOKS
from your library shelf

Call for Mr. Sniff
by Thomas P. Lewis (Harper & Row, 1981)
A good review of short *i* words while enjoying a story about Mr. Sniff.

Six Snowy Sheep
by Judith Ross Enderle (Boyds Mills, 1994)

Enjoy more antics of those silly sheep. This time they meet with disaster on a snowy day.

Snow Day
by Betsy Maestro (Scholastic, 1989)
After a snowstorm, a town is buried in snow until one by one people emerge to

dig their way out.

Super Snoop Sam Snout and the Case of the Missing Marble
by Anne LeMieux (Avon, 1994)
Super Snoot Sam solves the case of his friend Tommy's missing marble.

Exploring Letter/Sound Relationships

Explore Together

(A) • Buddy-read the *sn* book with a partner, identifying words that begin with /sn/*sn*.

• **Build-a-Word** • Provide cards with blend *sn* along with letter cards *a, e, i, o, k, c, p, w, r* to build and read words *snake, snap, snack, sneak, snip, snipe, snow, snore.* List the words and read together. Give clues about a word for children to guess. Examples: an animal with no legs (*snake*); breathe heavily while sleeping (*snore*); a light meal (*snack*); a bird with a very long bill (*snipe*).

• Recite the rhymes on right with children to reinforce the /sn/ sound. Encourage children to write their own rhymes and poems.

(A) • **Giant blend banner** • Write large letters *sn* on chart paper to top off the outline shape of a snowperson for children to draw and write words that begin with the blend *sn.* Display the banner and use as a resource for writing.

Poems, Rhymes, and Jingles

The snickering snail sneaked past the snoring snake.

Sneaky snowman snatched Snoopy's snazzy sneakers.

*Snowflakes, snowplows, snowmobiles, snow shovels, on a snowy day.
Snuggle inside and find a warm place to stay!*

Explore on Your Own

(A) • Provide sheets of paper for children to cut a long snake shape on which to draw and write words with initial blend /sn/*sn.* Tell children to use the Build-a-Word chart and blend banner to think of words to write in their books.

Using the *Blends and Digraphs* Activity Masters

Shoo, Crow! *and* **Missing Blends**
For additional practice with /sn/*sn,* engage children in the **manipulative** activities on pages 12 and 14.

Games and Puzzlers
To reinforce any letter/sound relationship, invite children to select one of the **interactive** ideas on pages 29–32.

Using (PM) Books Together

Alphabet Blends and Digraphs *sm, st, sp, sw*
Focus on words that have a variety of *s-* blends in the initial position.

Mom, Dad *(Starters One)*
Connect the content of the rhyme "Snoozing and snoring" to that in the *Starters* books about what moms and dads do. Review *-ing* words.

 performance assessment opportunities

 projects for *portfolios*

Sp as in spring

Make three columns on the chalkboard with heads *s, p, sp*. Write known words under each heading: *seven, sandwich, peas, potato, sponge, spoon*. [See *Alphabet Starters s, p.*] Give each child letter cards for *s* and *p*. Say words that begin with *s, p,* or *sp*. The child holds up one or both letter cards to show the beginning letter(s). Write the word in the column. Read the words and underline the letter(s) that represents the initial sound.

Developing Phonemic Awareness

Read the Rhyme
- Read the rhyme "All spotty," emphasizing the sound of the blend *sp* in the initial positions.
- Chant words *spotty, spent, spoon, sponged*. Discuss how the words are alike.

Find the Sound
- Show how the /sp/ sound is made in the mouth.
- Find something in the room whose name begins with /sp/ like *spoon*. Provide clues such as: change the beginning sound in *pool* to /sp/ and what word do you have? (*spool*); change the beginning sound in *soon* to /sp/ and what word do you have? (*spoon*).

Developing Print Awareness

Identify the Blend
- Write *spoon* on the chalkboard and ask children to identify the letters that stand for the beginning sound. Confirm that letters *sp* stand for the sound /sp/.
- Reread the rhyme "All spotty" and have children name the words they see that begin with the *sp* blend. Ask children what they think caused the spots.

Find the Blend
- **In the book** • Make the sound /sp/ as the letters *sp* are traced on page 1 of the book. Read the book together, looking at pictures and reinforcing /sp/ as you read the words.
- **Share a rhyme** • Volunteers can hold up the picture in the book as its name is said in the rhyme. Use the rhyme to focus on words that begin with the blend *sp*.

Sp *starts many words I know, like* sparklers *twinkling in the night,* sponges *to make things shiny bright, a* spider, *such a scary sight,* spots *I see in front of me, and a* spoon *I use to stir my tea.*

- Copy the rhyme onto chart paper. Read the rhyme together and underline words that begin with *sp*. Ask children to match each *sp* word in the rhyme with that in the book.
- Find additional words beginning with *sp* in print in the room. Read the words together to confirm that the /sp/ sound begins each word.

BOOKS
from your library shelf

Itsy-Bitsy Spider
by Iza Trapani (Whispering Coyote, 1994)
The song about the spider is taken to new heights as the spider travels all over the house.

Miss Spider's Tea Party
By David Kirk (Scholastic, 1994)
In this unusual counting book, Miss Spider wants to have a smashing tea party but everyone declines. Children's Choice.

Oodles of Noodles
by J. and L. Hymes
(Young Scott Books, 1964)
In this collection of poems, focus on "Spinach." The author lists a series of words beginning with /sp/.

Exploring Letter/Sound Relationships

Explore Together

 • Buddy-read the *sp* book with a partner, identifying words that begin with /sp/*sp*.

• **Spaceship** • Draw a giant spaceship on the chalkboard. Inside the ship write the following words, scrambling the letters: *spider, sponge, sparrow, spoon, spin, sport, spool, spot, spit, spout, speak.* Volunteers can choose a word to rewrite and read.

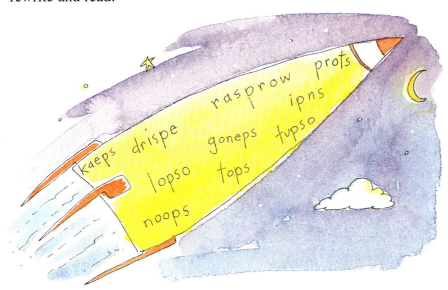

• Recite the rhymes on right with children to reinforce the /sp/ sound. Encourage children to write their own rhymes and poems.

 • **Giant blend banner** • Write large letters *sp* on chart paper for children to draw and write words that begin with the blend /sp/*sp*. Display the banner and use as a resource for writing.

Explore on Your Own

 • Provide blank round-shape books for children to draw and write words with initial blend *sp*. Children can add eight lengths of yarn to the cover to resemble a spider. Tell children to use the blend banner to think of words to write in their books.

Using the *Blends and Digraphs* Activity Masters

Shoo, Crow!, Missing Blends, *and* Race to the Web
For additional practice with /sp/*sp*, engage children in the **manipulative** activities on pages 12, 14, and 25.

Games and Puzzlers
To reinforce any letter/sound relationship, invite children to select one of the **interactive** ideas on pages 29–32.

Poems, Rhymes, and Jingles

The itsy-bitsy spider sped up the water spout.
Out came the rain and washed the spider out.
Out came the sun and dried up all the rain,
Then the itsy-bitsy spider sped up the spout again.

Hey diddle, diddle,
the cat and the fiddle,
The cow jumped over the moon;
The little dog laughed to see such a sport,
And the dish ran away with the spoon.

Using **PM** Books Together

Alphabet Blends and Digraphs *sc, sk, sl, sm, sn, st* Focus on words that have a variety of *s*- blends in the initial position.

Packing my bag
(Starters Two)
Recall the surprise item packed in a boy's bag.

 performance assessment opportunities

 projects for *portfolios*

spr *as in sprouts*

Tips for the English Language Learner

Make three columns on the chalkboard with heads *s, sp, spr.* Write known words under each heading: *sun, socks; spider, spoon; sprouts, spring.* [See *Alphabet Starters s and Alphabet Blends and Digraphs sp.*] Give each child letter cards for *s, p, r.* Say words that begin with *s, sp,* or *spr.* The child holds up one, two, or all three letter cards to show the beginning letter(s). Write the word in the column. Read the words and underline the letter(s) that represents the initial sound.

Developing Phonemic Awareness

Read the Rhyme
- Read the rhyme "The garden sprinkler," emphasizing the sound of the blend *spr* in the initial positions.
- Chant words *sprinkler, sprays, sprouts, spread, spring.* Discuss how the words are alike.

Find the Sound
- Show how the /spr/ sound is made in the mouth.
- **(A)** • Find something in the room whose name begins with /spr/ like bean or Brussels *sprouts.* Provide clues such as: the name of a season that rhymes with *ring* (*spring*); to open wide your arms and the word rhymes with *red* (*spread*).

Developing Print Awareness

Identify the Blend
- Write *sprouts* on the chalkboard and ask children to identify the letters that stand for the beginning sound. Confirm that letters *spr* stand for the sound /spr/.
- Reread the rhyme "The garden sprinkler" and have children name the words they see that begin with the *spr* blend.

Find the Blend
- **In the book** • Make the sound /spr/ as the letters *spr* are traced on page 1 in the book. Read the book together, looking at pictures and emphasizing /spr/ as you read the words.
- **(A)** • **Share a rhyme** • Volunteers can hold up the picture in the book as its name is said in the rhyme. Use the rhyme to focus on words that begin with the blend *spr.*

> *What does* spr *start?*
> A sprinkler *for the lawn,*
> *a bouncy* spring,
> *a* spray *from a can,*
> *or the* spray *of the sea—*
> *and* sprouts *for me.*

- Copy the rhyme onto chart paper. Read the rhyme together and underline words that begin with *spr.* Ask children to match each *spr* word in the rhyme with that in the book.
- Find additional words beginning with *spr* in print in the room. Read the words together to confirm that the /spr/ sound begins each word.

BOOKS
from your library shelf

Spring
by Ron Hirschi (Cobblehill, 1990)
This photographic tribute to spring captures spring flowers sprouting and other wonders of nature.

Spring Green
by Valrie M. Selkowe
(Lothrop, Lee & Shepard, 1985)
It's spring and time for woodchuck's party. There is a prize for the one who brings the best green thing. [Focus on words with *r* blends.]

Exploring Letter/Sound Relationships

Explore Together

(A) • Buddy-read the *spr* book with a partner, identifying words that begin with /spr/*spr.*
• **Build-a-Word** • Write words on the chalkboard: *rain, rang, ray, read, ring, rung.* Children add *sp* to the beginning of each word and read the new word. Then they can copy a *spr* word from the chalkboard, scramble the letters, and ask a partner to rewrite and read.

• Recite the rhymes on right with children to reinforce the /spr/ sound. Encourage children to write their own rhymes and poems.
(A) • **Giant blend banner** • Write large letters *spr* on chart paper for children to draw and write words that begin with the blend *spr.* Display the banner and use as a resource for writing.

Explore on Your Own

(A) • Provide blank books for children to draw and write words with initial blend /spr/*spr.* Tell children to use the Build-a-Word chart and blend banner to think of words to write in their books.

Using the *Blends and Digraphs* Activity Masters

Building Blocks *and* Race to the Web
For additional practice with /spr/*spr,* engage children in the **manipulative** activities on pages 24 and 25.

Games and Puzzlers
To reinforce any letter/sound relationship, invite children to select one of the **interactive** ideas on pages 29–32.

 performance assessment opportunities

 projects for *portfolios*

Poems, Rhymes, and Jingles

Sprinklers sprout spring seeds.

*Jack Sprat could eat no fat;
His wife could eat no lean.
And so between them both, you see,
They licked the platter clean.
Jack Sprat likes vegetables;
His wife likes fatty meat.
So with a platter of sprouts and chops,
They both had plenty to eat.*

Using **PM** Books Together

Alphabet Blends and Digraphs *sp, pr* Show how the initial sound in words change when adding a letter. Change from *sp* to *spr* and from *pr* to *spr.*

Where are the babies? *(Starters Two)* Animal babies are often born in spring.

squ as in squirrel

Developing Phonemic Awareness

Read the Rhyme

• Read the rhyme "Orange squash," emphasizing the sound of the blend *squ* in the initial positions.
• Chant words *squash, squeeze, squirt.* Discuss how the words are alike.

Find the Sound

• Show how the /skw/ sound is made in the mouth.
A • Find something in the room whose name begins with /skw/ like *squash.* Provide clues such as: the shape of a box (*square*); to crouch with the knees bent (*squat*).

Developing Print Awareness

Identify the Blend

• Write *squash* on the chalkboard and ask children to identify the letters that stand for the beginning sound. Confirm that letters *squ* stand for the sound /skw/.
• Reread the rhyme "Orange squash" and have children name the words they see that begin with the *squ* blend.

Find the Blend

• **In the book** • Make the sound /skw/ as the letters squ are traced on page 1 in the book. Read the book together, looking at pictures and emphasizing /skw/ as you read the words.
A • **Share a rhyme** • Volunteers can hold up the picture in the book as its name is said in the rhyme. Use the rhyme to focus on words that begin with the blend *squ.*

> *What can you do with* squ?
> *You can start the word* squiggle;
> *You can start* squash *too,*
> *but there's more you can do with* squ.
> A squirrel *in a tree,*
> a squid *in the sea,*
> *and a four-sided* square
> *start with* squ *too!*

• Copy the rhyme onto chart paper. Read the rhyme together and underline words that begin with *squ.* Ask children to match each *squ* word in the rhyme with that in the book.
• Find additional words beginning with *squ* in print in the room. Read the words together to confirm that the /skw/ sound begins each word.

BOOKS
from your library shelf

Squares
by Arnold Shapiro (Dial, 1992)
Each double-page spread opens up to a square object for children to name.

Cook
by Paul Manning (Macmillan, 1988)

A squirrel bakes a chocolate cake to share.

We Watch Squirrels
by Ada and Frank Graham
(Dodd Mead. 1985)
Children learn of the habits, actions, and habitat of the gray squirrel.

Nuts to You
By Lois Ehlert (Harcourt Brace, 1993)
A squirrel visits the author's home.

Exploring Letter/Sound Relationships

Explore Together

Ⓐ • Buddy-read the *squ* book with a partner, identifying words that begin with /skw/*squ.*

• **Build-a-Word** • Write words on the board: *square, squash, squat, squeal, squid, squeeze, squirrel.* Children can trace over letters *squ* and read the words. Give clues for word identification: word that rhymes with *share;* a yellow or green vegetable; animal with a furry tail; to crouch with the knees bent; word that rhymes with *tease;* sound a pig makes; a sea animal like an octopus but with ten arms.

• Recite the rhymes on right with children to reinforce the /skw/ sound. Encourage children to write their own rhymes and poems.

Ⓐ • **Giant blend banner** • Write large letters *squ* on chart paper for children to draw and write words that begin with the blend *squ.* Display the banner and use as a resource for writing.

Explore on Your Own

Ⓐ • Provide blank squirrel-shape books for children to draw and write words with initial blend *squ.* Tell children to use the Build-a-Word chart and blend banner to think of words to write in their books.

Poems, Rhymes, and Jingles

A squad of squids squiggles and squirms.

Squeaky squirrel squeezes squash.

Squishy, squashy, squishy, squashy, I walked in a shower of rain. I stepped in a puddle right up to my middle. Squishy, squashy all over again!

Using Ⓟⓜ Books Together

Alphabet Blends and Digraphs *sk* Compare words that begin with blends *sk* and *squ.*

Using the *Blends and Digraphs* Activity Masters

Building Blocks
For additional practice with /skw/*squ,* engage children in the **manipulative** activity on page 24.

Games and Puzzlers
To reinforce any letter/sound relationship, invite children to select one of the **interactive** ideas on pages 29–32.

Ⓐ *performance assessment* opportunities

 projects for *portfolios*

st as in stamps

Tips for the English Language Learner

Help children understand how sounds are blended together and how leaving out or adding a letter changes a word. Write words on the chalkboard. Children can choose a word to read, add initial *s* to change the initial sound from /t/ to /st/, and then read the new word. Use words: *tab, tack, take, tale, talk, tall, tar, tart, team, tick, tone, top, tore.*

Developing Phonemic Awareness

Read the Rhyme
- Read the rhyme "Stop, stand still!," emphasizing the sound of the blend *st* in the initial positions.
- Chant words *stop, stand, still.* Discuss how the words are alike.

Find the Sound
- Show how the /st/ sound is made in the mouth.
- **(A)** Find something in the room whose name begins with /st/ like *stop.* Provide clues such as: the part of a flower that holds the blossom and leaves (*stem*); a seat with no back or arms (*stool*).

Developing Print Awareness

Identify the Blend
- Write *stop* on the chalkboard and ask children to identify the letters that stand for the beginning sound. Confirm that letters *st* stand for the sound /st/.
- Reread the rhyme "Stop, stand still!" and have children name the words they see that begin with the *st* blend.

Find the Blend
- **In the book** • Make the sound /st/ as the letters *st* are traced on page 1 of the book. Read the book together, looking at pictures and reinforcing /st/ as you read the words.
- **(A)** • **Share a rhyme** • Volunteers can hold up the picture in the book as its name is said in the rhyme. Use the rhyme to focus on words that begin with the blend *st.*

> Stop *and look, find the* stars *in your book.*
> *Find* stamps *to put on letters*
> *and* steps *throughout the town.*
> *Find* stones *in all colors and sizes*
> *and a* stool *for sitting down.*

- Copy the rhyme onto chart paper. Read the rhyme together and underline words that begin with *st.* Ask children to match each *st* word in the rhyme with that in the book.
- Find additional words beginning with *st* in print in the room. Read the words together to confirm that the /st/ sound begins each word.

BOOKS
from your library shelf

The Stinky Cheese Man and Other Fairly Stupid Tales
by Jon Scieszka (Viking Penguin, 1992)
This is a zany collection of revised fairy tales children will enjoy. Caldecott Honor Book.

Stone Soup
retold by John Warren Stewig
(Holiday House, 1991)
In this version of the old soup-from-a-stone tale, a girl named Grethel is the one who gets the selfish villagers to give up their vegetables and beef shank for the soup pot.

Draw Me a Star
by Eric Carle (Philomel, 1992)
This is a circular story beginning with a young boy at his easel painting a star. Each thing in turn asks for something else, only to end with the star.

Exploring Letter/Sound Relationships

Explore Together

Ⓐ • Buddy-read the *st* book with a partner, identifying words that begin with /st/*st*.
• **Starring *st*** • Cut star shapes from yellow construction paper. Write a word on each star. Include some words that begin with *st* and some that do not. Children choose a star to read. If the word begins like *star,* the word can be pinned onto a bulletin board that has been covered with blue paper. Then read all the star words together on the board.

• Recite the rhymes on right with children to reinforce the /st/ sound. Encourage children to write their own rhymes and poems.
Ⓐ • **Giant blend banner** • Write large letters *st* on chart paper for children to draw and write words that begin with the blend *st*. Display the banner and use as a resource for writing.

Explore on Your Own

🅰 • Provide blank star-shape books for children to draw and write words with initial blend *st*. Tell children to use the star bulletin board and the banner to think of words to write in their books.

Poems, Rhymes, and Jingles

A stout stegosaurus stomped on the stagecoach.

Star light, star bright,
First star I see tonight,
I wish I may, I wish I might,
Have the wish I wish tonight.

Step on a crack,
You'll strain your back.
Step in a hole,
You'll break your best bowl.
Step in a ditch,
Your nose will start to itch.
Step in the dirt,
You'll stain your new shirt.

Using 🅿ⓜ Books Together

Alphabet Blends and Digraphs *str* Compare and group words with initial blends *st* and *str*.

Stop! *(Starters Two)* The themes for both Stop! and the rhyme "Stop, stand still!" focus on street safety.

Using the *Blends and Digraphs* Activity Masters

Missing Blends *and* Stars and Stripes
For additional practice with /st/*st,* engage children in the **manipulative** activities on pages 14 and 26.

Games and Puzzlers
To reinforce any letter/sound relationship, invite children to select one of the **interactive** ideas on pages 29–32.

Ⓐ *performance assessment* opportunities

🅰 projects for *portfolios*

Blends and Digraphs **55**

str *as in string*

Show how known sounds can blend together to make new sounds. Write words on chalkboard: *ring, ripe, range, rain, raw, ride, ripe.* Review initial sound /r/ and read the words. Review the /st/ sound and add letters *st* to each word. Read the new words with initial /str/.

Developing Phonemic Awareness

Read the Rhyme

- Read the rhyme "Striding and stretching," emphasizing the sound of the blend *str* in the initial positions.
- Chant words *striding, stretching, stride, strong, street, stretch.* Discuss how the words are alike.

Find the Sound

- Show how the /str/ sound is made in the mouth.
- **A** Find something in the room whose name begins with /str/ like *stride.* Provide clues such as: something we use at lunchtime to drink milk or juice with (*straw*); something we use for tying or wrapping (*string*).

Developing Print Awareness

Identify the Blend

- Write *stride* on the chalkboard and ask children to identify the letters that stand for the beginning sound. Confirm that letters *str* stand for the sound /str/.
- Reread the rhyme "Striding and stretching" and have children name the words they see that begin with the *str* blend. Ask children to demonstrate *stretching* as they *stride.*

Find the Blend

- **In the book** • Make the sound /str/ as the letters *str* are traced on page 1 in the book. Read the book together, looking at pictures and reinforcing /str/ as you read the words.
- **A** • **Share a rhyme** • Volunteers can hold up the picture in the book as its name is said in the rhyme. Use the rhyme to focus on words that begin with the *str* blend.

  > *Where can you find* str *words?*
  > *Just take a look and think.*
  > *Look for* straw *in a cool drink.*
  > *Look for* street *in a city or town.*
  > *Look for* stripes *going across or up and down.*
  > *Look for* strawberries *in jam; take a bite!*
  > *Look for* string *in a ball or on a kite.*

- Copy the rhyme onto chart paper. Read the rhyme together and underline words that begin with *str.* Ask children to match each *str* word in the rhyme with that in the book.
- Find additional words beginning with *str* in print in the room. Read the words together to confirm that the /str/ sound begins each word.

Strawberry
by Jennifer Coldrey (Silver Burdett/Stopwatch Books, 1989)
The growth cycle of a strawberry plant is described in simple text enhanced by photos and line drawings.

The Strawflower
by Hilde Heyduck-Huth (Margaret McElderry, 1987)
Have children heard of a strawflower? The one in this story travels from its bouquet through a snowstorm to a snowman family, and then into a girl's home.

Strega Nona's Magic Lessons
by Tomie de Paola (Harcourt Brace, 1982)
Strega Nona is a favorite character who appears in a series of humorous tales.

Exploring Letter/Sound Relationships

Explore Together

(A) • Buddy-read the *str* book with a partner, identifying words that begin with /str/*str*.

• **Build-a-Word** • Provide cards with blend *str* along with letter cards *a, e, i, o, u, n, g, m, k* to build and read words *string, strong, strung, strap, stripe, strange, streak, stream, strum, strain, strike.* List the words and read together.

• Recite the rhymes on right with children to reinforce the /str/ sound. Encourage children to write their own rhymes and poems.

(A) • **Giant blend banner** • Write large letters *str* on chart paper for children to draw and write words that begin with the blend *str.* Display the banner and use as a resource for writing.

Explore on Your Own

(A) • Provide blank strawberry-shape books for children to draw and write words with initial blend /str/*str.* Tell children to use the Build-a-Word chart and blend banner to think of words to write in their books.

stripes   strum

Using PM Books Together

Alphabet Blends and Digraphs *scr, spr*
Compare and group words with three-letter blends with *-r.*

We can run
(Starters Two)
Add sentence pairs to the story about moving children and animals, using words *stride, stretch.*

Using the *Blends and Digraphs* Activity Masters

Building Blocks *and* Stars and Stripes
For additional practice with /str/*str,* engage children in the **manipulative** activities on pages 24 and 26.

Games and Puzzlers
To reinforce any letter/sound relationship, invite children to select one of the **interactive** ideas on pages 29–32.

 performance assessment opportunities

 projects for *portfolios*

SW *as in swan*

Tips for the English Language Learner

Write words on the chalkboard: *wear, weep, way, warm, well, wing, wish, witch.* Read the words together. Make new words by having children add the letter *s* to each and then read the new *sw* word.

Developing Phonemic Awareness

Read the Rhyme
- Read the rhyme "Welcome swallows," emphasizing the sound of the blend *sw* in the initial positions.
- Chant words *swallows, swerve, swoop, swing, swamp, swift.* Discuss how the words are alike.

Find the Sound
- Show how the /sw/ sound is made in the mouth.
- **A** • Find something in the room whose name begins with /sw/ like *swan.* Provide clues such as: playground equipment you play on (*swings*); a knitted piece of clothing you wear to keep warm (*sweater*).

Developing Print Awareness

Identify the Blend
- Write *swallows* on the chalkboard and ask children to identify the letters that stand for the beginning sound. Confirm that letters *sw* stand for the sound /sw/.
- Reread the rhyme "Welcome swallows" and have children name the words they see that begin with the *sw* blend.

Find the Blend
- **In the book** • Make the sound /sw/ as the letters *sw* are traced on page 1 of the book. Read the book together, looking at pictures and emphasizing /sw/ as you read the words.
- **A** • **Share a rhyme** • Volunteers can hold up the picture in the book as its name is said in the rhyme. Use the rhyme to focus on words that begin with the blend *sw.*

> *Let's look for* sw.
> *Turn on the* switch!
> *We see the blend in* swamp
> *and in* swimming pool *too.*
> *It's flying high in* swings
> *and have you heard…*
> sw *starts* swan, *the loveliest of birds.*

- Copy the rhyme onto chart paper. Read the rhyme together and underline words that begin with *sw.* Ask children to match each *sw* word in the rhyme with that in the book.
- Find additional words beginning with *sw* in print in the room. Read the words together to confirm that the /sw/ sound begins each word.

BOOKS
from your library shelf

Over the Steamy Swamp
by Paul Geraghty (Harcourt Brace, 1989)
A steamy swamp is the setting for this circular cumulative tale with a food chain theme.

Seasons of Swans
by Monica Wellington (Dutton, 1990)
This is a realistic story of two swans living on Willow Pond. It portrays the behavior of swans and how they care for their young.

Switch On, Switch Off
by Melvin Berger (Thomas Y. Crowell, 1989)
This is a Let's-Read-and-Find-Out-Science Book about electricity. Notable Children's Trade Books in Science 1989.

Exploring Letter/Sound Relationships

Explore Together

 • Buddy-read the *sw* book with a partner, identifying words that begin with /sw/*sw*.

- **Build-a-Word** • Provide cards with blend *sw* along with letter cards *i, a, m, p, n, g, y* to build and read words *swim, swam, swamp, swan, swing, sway*. List the words and read together.

- Recite the rhymes on right with children to reinforce the /sw/ sound. Encourage children to write their own rhymes and poems.

 • **Giant blend banner** • Write large letters *sw* on chart paper for children to draw and write words that begin with the blend *sw*. Display the banner and use as a resource for writing.

Explore on Your Own

 • Provide blank swan-shape books for children to draw and write words with initial blend /sw/*sw*. Tell children to use the Build-a-Word chart and blend banner to think of words to write in their books.

Using the *Blends and Digraphs* Activity Masters

Dot-to-Dot
For additional practice with /sw/*sw*, engage children in the **manipulative** activity on page 15.

Games and Puzzlers
To reinforce any letter/sound relationship, invite children to select one of the **interactive** ideas on pages 29–32.

 performance assessment opportunities

 projects for *portfolios*

Blends and Digraphs **59**

Poems, Rhymes, and Jingles

Swan swam over the sea,
Swim, swan, swim!
Swan swam back again,
Well swum, swan!

Sweep, sweep,
chimney sweep,
From the bottom to the top.
Sweep it all up,
chimney sweep,
From the bottom to the top.

Using **PM** Books Together

Alphabet Blends and Digraphs *tw* Focus on words that have variant -*w* blends in the initial position.

We can run
(Starters Two)
Use story language to write about additional animals that *swim, sway, swerve, swoop,* or *swing*.

th as in thumb

To help distinguish between the sounds of /t/ and /th/, make three columns on the chalkboard with heads *t, h, th*. Write known words under each heading: *tent, teeth, hand, horse, thumb, thimble*. [Refer to *Alphabet Starters t, h*.] Give each child letter cards for *t* and *h*. Say words that begin with *t, h*, or *th*. The child holds up one or both letter cards to show the beginning letter(s). Write the word in the column. Read the words and underline the letter(s) that represents the initial sound. Examples: *torn, horn, thorn, tank, Hank, thank, tin, thin.*

Developing Phonemic Awareness

Read the Rhyme

- Read the rhyme "Thudding and thumping," emphasizing the sound of the digraph *th* in initial positions.
- Move about like hopping rabbits as you chant words *thudding, thumping, thumpity, thump, thuds*. Discuss how the words are alike.

Find the Sound

- Show how the /th/ sound is made in the mouth.
- Ⓐ Find something in the room whose name begins with /th/ like *thumpity thump*. Provide clues such as: the number that follows twelve (*thirteen*); twenty-nine (*thirty*); nine hundred ninety-nine (*one thousand*).

Developing Print Awareness

Identify the Digraph

- Write *thumpity thump* on the chalkboard and ask children to identify the letters that stand for the beginning sound in each word. Confirm that letters *th* stand for the sound /th/.
- Reread the rhyme "Thudding and thumping" and have children name the words they see that begin with the *th* digraph.

Find the Digraph

- **In the book** • Make the sound /th/ as the letters *th* are traced on page 1 of the book. Read the book together, looking at pictures and emphasizing /th/ as you read the words.
- Ⓐ **Share a rhyme** • Volunteers can hold up the picture in the book as its name is said in the rhyme. Use the rhyme to focus on words that begin with the digraph *th*.

> *Think about words that start with* th—
> thistle, *a plant with blooms purple or red*
> *and* thorn, *a sharp point found on a stem.*
> *You'll want a* thimble *on your* thumb
> *the next time you sew*
> *and a* thermometer *to see*
> *how far your temperature goes.*

- Copy the rhyme onto chart paper. Read the rhyme together and underline words that begin with *th*. Ask children to match each *th* word in the rhyme with that in the book.
- Find additional words beginning with *th* in print in the room. Read the words together to confirm that the /th/ sound begins each word.

BOOKS
from your library shelf

Thump, Thump, Rat-a-Tat-Tat
by Gene Baer (Harper & Row, 1989)
A marching band boldly marches toward the reader with vibrant colors and rhythmic cadence.

Thunder Cake
by Patricia Polacco (Philomel, 1990)
A grandmother's solution to her granddaughter's fear of the storm is bake a thunder cake.

Thumbelina
by Hans Christian Andersen, retold by James Riordan (G. P. Putnam's , 1991)
This is a beautifully illustrated retelling of the timeless tale of a character no bigger than a thumb.

Exploring Letter/Sound Relationships

Explore Together

Ⓐ • Buddy-read the *th* book with a partner, identifying words that begin with /th/*th*.
• **Build-a-Word** • Provide cards with digraph *th* along with letter cards *a, i, o, c, k, n, g, r, d* to build and read words *thick, thin, thing, think, thank, thorn, third.* List the words and read together.

• Recite the rhymes on right with children to reinforce the /th/ sound. Encourage children to write their own rhymes and poems.
Ⓐ • **Giant digraph banner** • Write large letters *th* on chart paper for children to draw and write words that begin with the digraph *th*. Display the banner and use as a resource for writing.

Poems, Rhymes, and Jingles

I thought the thunder thumped a thousand times on Thursday.

Thirty days has September, April, June, and November; all the rest have thirty-one, excepting February alone, and that has twenty-eight days clear and twenty-nine in each leap year.

th Thursday think thorn

Explore on Your Own

Ⓐ • Provide blank books for children to draw and write words with initial digraph *th*. Tell children to use the Build-a-Word chart and digraph banner to think of words to write in their books.

Using the *Blends and Digraphs* Activity Masters

Word Shapes, Digraph Dominoes, *and* King Theo
For additional practice with /th/*th*, engage children in the **manipulative** activities on pages 21, 22–23, and 28.

Games and Puzzlers
To reinforce any letter/sound relationship, invite children to select one of the **interactive** ideas on pages 29–32.

Using Ⓟⓜ Books Together

Alphabet Blends and Digraphs *sh, ph, wh, ch*
Focus on words that have a variety of digraphs in the initial position.

We can run
(Starters Two)
Focus on animals that move by thumping and thudding. Children can demonstrate.

 performance assessment opportunities

 projects for *portfolios*

thr *as in thread*

Make three columns on the chalkboard with heads *th, r, thr.* Write known words under each heading: *thumb, thimble, rabbit, river, three, thread.* [See *Alphabet Starters r* and *Alphabet Blends and Digraphs th.*] Give each child letter cards for *t, h,* and *r.* Say words that begin with *r, th,* or *thr.* The child holds up one, two, or all three letter cards to show the beginning letter(s). Write the word in the column. Read the words and underline the letter(s) that represents the initial sound.

Developing Phonemic Awareness

Read the Rhyme
• Read the rhyme "Three baby thrushes," emphasizing the sound of the blend *thr* in the initial positions.
• Chant words *three, thrushes, throats.* Discuss how the words are alike.

Find the Sound
• Show how the /thr/ sound is made in the mouth.
(A) • Find something in the room whose name begins with /thr/ like *three thrushes.* Provide clues such as: a word that starts with /thr/ and rhymes with *new* (*threw*); a word that starts with /thr/ and rhymes with *boat* (*throat*).

Developing Print Awareness

Identify the Blend
• Write *three thrushes* on the chalkboard and ask children to identify the letters that stand for the beginning sound. Confirm that letters *thr* stand for the sound /thr/.
• Reread the rhyme "Three baby thrushes" and have children name the words they see that begin with the *thr* blend.

Find the Blend
• **In the book** • Make the sound /thr/ as the letters *thr* are traced on page 1 in the book. Read the book together, looking at pictures and emphasizing /thr/ as you read the words.
(A) • **Share a rhyme** • Volunteers can hold up the picture in the book as its name is said in the rhyme. Use the rhyme to focus on words that begin with the blend *thr.*

> T,h,r, *the letters* three,
> *start these words as you will see:*
> *There is* thread *on a spool,*
> *a* throne *for a king,*
> *a* throat *that's sore,*
> *and* throw *is one more.*

• Copy the rhyme onto chart paper. Read the rhyme together and underline words that begin with *thr.* Ask children to match each *thr* word in the rhyme with that in the book.
• Find additional words beginning with *thr* in print in the room. Read the words together to confirm that the /thr/ sound begins each word.

BOOKS
from your library shelf

Three Little Kittens
by Paul Galdone (Clarion, 1986)
This is a new version of a favorite rhyme
about three kittens and their lost mittens.

Three Hat Day
by Laura Geringer (Harper & Row, 1987)
R. R. Pottle has a passion for hats, often
wearing more than one a day.
ALA Notable Children's Book.

Three Cheers for Hippo
by John Stadler (Thomas Y. Crowell, 1987)
Pig and Dog are thrilled to go with Hippo
for a parachuting lesson. Cat is terrified.
Three hungry alligators wait below to gob-
ble up the jumpers.

Exploring Letter/Sound Relationships

Explore Together

(A) • Buddy-read the *thr* book with a partner, identifying words that begin with
/thr/*thr*.

• **Word scramble** • Write these words on the chalkboard, scrambling the letters:
thread, thrill, three, throat, throne, throw. Give partners a word to unscramble
and rewrite on the chalkboard.

• Read the words together.

• Recite the rhymes on right with children to reinforce the /thr/ sound. Encourage
children to write their own rhymes and poems.

(A) • **Giant blend banner** • Write large letters *thr* on chart paper for children to
draw and write words that begin with the blend *thr.* Display the banner and use
as a resource for writing.

Explore on Your Own

(A) • Provide blank books with three pages for children to draw and write words
with initial blend /thr/*thr.* Tell children to use the blend banner to think of
words to write in their books.

Using (PM) Books Together

**Alphabet Blends and
Digraphs** *th* Compare the
sounds of /th/ and /thr/ in
initial positions in words.

Can you see the eggs?
(Starters Two)
Connect the themes of the
story with the rhyme
"Three baby thrushes," to
focus on egg-bearing
animal mothers.

Using the *Blends and Digraphs* Activity Masters

**Building Blocks *and*
King Theo**
For additional practice with /thr/*thr,*
engage children in the **manipulative**
activities on pages 24 and 28.

Games and Puzzlers
To reinforce any letter/sound relationship, invite children to select
one of the **interactive** ideas on
pages 29–32.

 performance assessment opportunities

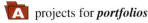 projects for *portfolios*

tr *as in tree*

Developing Phonemic Awareness

Read the Rhyme

- Read the rhyme "Taking trips," emphasizing the sound of the blend *tr* in the initial positions.
- Chant words *trips, travel, train, tractor, truck, trike*. Discuss how the words are alike.

Find the Sound

- Show how the /tr/ sound is made in the mouth.
- (A) Find something in the room whose name begins with /tr/ like *train*. Provide clues such as: change the beginning sound in *way* to /tr/, and what word do you have? (*tray*); change the beginning sound in *me* to /tr/ and what word do you have? (*tree*)

Developing Print Awareness

Identify the Blend

- Write *train* on the chalkboard and ask children to identify the letters that stand for the beginning sound. Confirm that letters *tr* stand for the sound /tr/.
- Reread the rhyme "Taking trips" and have children name the words they see that begin with the *tr* blend. How do they travel?

Find the Blend

- **In the book** • Make the sound /tr/ as the letters *tr* are traced on page 1 of the book. Read the book together, looking at pictures and reinforcing /tr/ as you read the words.
- (A) **Share a rhyme** • Volunteers can hold up the picture in the book as its name is said in the rhyme. Use the rhyme to focus on words that begin with the blend *tr*.

  Tr *is for a* tractor *on the farm,*
  a triangle *shape,*
  a train *with a load,*
  a tree *in a field,*
  and a truck *on the road.*

- Copy the rhyme onto chart paper. Read the rhyme together and underline words that begin with *tr*. Ask children to match each *tr* word in the rhyme with that in the book.
- Find additional words beginning with *tr* in print in the room. Read the words together to confirm that the /tr/ sound begins each word.

triangle

Exploring Letter/Sound Relationships

Explore Together

(A) • Buddy-read the *tr* book with a partner, identifying words that begin with /tr/*tr*.

• **Trail of words** • Mark a trail for children to follow in the classroom. Along the trail will be word cards featuring the blend *tr*. Use words *trace, track, tractor, trade, trail, train, trap, travel, trash, tray, treat, tree, trick, try, trim, trip, troop, trot, true, trunk*. Children read words along the trail, ending with a treasure chest of treats for children to share.

• Recite the rhymes on right with children to reinforce the /tr/ sound. Encourage children to write their own rhymes and poems.

(A) • **Giant blend banner** • Write large letters *tr* within the shape of a treasure chest on chart paper for children to draw and write words that begin with the blend *tr*. Display the banner and use as a resource for writing.

Explore on Your Own

(A) • Provide blank tree-shape books for children to draw and write words with initial blend /tr/*tr*. Tell children to use the blend banner to think of words to write in their books.

Using the *Blends and Digraphs* Activity Masters

Hidden Pictures *and* Pretty Presents
For additional practice with /tr/*tr*, engage children in the **manipulative** activities on pages 7 and 8.

Games and Puzzlers
To reinforce any letter/sound relationship, invite children to select one of the **interactive** ideas on pages 29–32.

 performance assessment opportunities

 projects for *portfolios*

Poems, Rhymes, and Jingles

Troy travels on trains, trucks, and trolleys.

The trail to the treasure was traced to the tree.

*A peanut sat on the railroad track,
Its heart was all a-flutter;
Choo-choo train travels around the bend,
Toot toot!
Peanut butter!*

Using **PM** Books Together

Alphabet Blends and Digraphs *thr* Compare and group words with initial blends *tr* and *thr*.

The way I go to school (*Starters One*) Add sentences to the story using words *train, trolley, truck*.

tw as in twins

Tips for the
English Language Learner

Focus on isolating initial sounds in words. Have children change the beginning sound in each word to /tw/ and say the new word. Write the new words on the chalkboard. Use words: *nice (twice), wig (twig), win (twin), fine (twine), wrinkle (twinkle), girl (twirl), list (twist).*

Developing Phonemic Awareness

Read the Rhyme
• Read the rhyme "The twins are twirling," emphasizing the sound of the blend *tw* in the initial positions.
• Chant words *twins, twirling, twisting, twinkling.* Discuss how the words are alike.

Find the Sound
• Show how the /tw/ sound is made in the mouth.
Ⓐ • Find something in the room whose name begins with /tw/ like *twist.* Provide clues such as: a small branch of a tree (*twig*); the answer for six plus six (*twelve*).

Developing Print Awareness

Identify the Blend
• Write *twins* on the chalkboard and ask children to identify the letters that stand for the beginning sound. Confirm that letters *tw* stand for the sound /tw/.
• Reread the rhyme "The twins are twirling" and have children name the words they see that begin with the *tw* blend.

Find the Blend
• **In the book** • Make the sound /tw/ as the letters *tw* are traced on page 1 of the book. Read the book together, looking at pictures and reinforcing /tw/ as you read the words.
Ⓐ • **Share a rhyme** • Volunteers can hold up the picture in the book as its name is said in the rhyme. Use the rhyme to focus on words that begin with the blend *tw.*

> *Point to the start of* twist, *and what do you see?*
> *The blend* tw. *Where else can it be?*
> *At the start of* twins *and* twigs *and, then again,*
> *You will see* tw *in* two *numbers over ten.*
> Tw *appears in* twelve *and in* twenty *once again.*

• Copy the rhyme onto chart paper. Read the rhyme together and underline words that begin with *tw.* Ask children to match each *tw* word in the rhyme with that in the book.
• Find additional words beginning with *tw* in print in the room. Read the words together to confirm that the /tw/ sound begins each word.

BOOKS
from your library shelf

Twinkle, Twinkle, Little Star
by Jane Taylor (Morrow, 1992)
A star path guides two children from their nursery room window up into a cloud-borne sailing ship.

The Twelve Dancing Princesses
by Freya Littledale (Scholastic, 1988)
This is a retelling of the Grimm tale about twelve enchanted princesses. Notable 1989 Childrens Trade Books in the Field of Social Studies.

Walking to the Creek
by David Williams (Alfred A. Knopf, 1990)
Twin boys visit their grandparents and hike to the creek near the farm.

Exploring Letter/Sound Relationships

Explore Together

A • Buddy-read the *tw* book with a partner, identifying words that begin with /tw/*tw*.

• **Build-a-Word** • Provide cards with blend *tw* along with letter cards *i, g, n, s, t, r, l, e* to build and read words *twig, twin, twist, twirl, twine.* List the words and read together.

Poems, Rhymes, and Jingles

Twelve twisted twigs twined around the tree.

Twenty stars twinkle at twilight.

Twins Tweedledum and Tweedledee agreed to take a vote To decide which twin should get the fancy new tweed coat. Tweedledum said Tweedledee has twelve coats already. So Tweedledum was to get the new tweed coat on Friday.

• Recite the rhymes on right with children to reinforce the /tw/ sound. Encourage children to write their own rhymes and poems.

A • **Giant blend banner** • Write large letters *tw* on chart paper for children to draw and write words that begin with the blend *tw*. Display the banner and use as a resource for writing.

Explore on Your Own

A • Provide blank books for children to draw and write words with initial blend *tw*. Tell children to use the Build-a-Word chart and blend banner to think of words to write in their books. Add construction paper covers. Children can write the letters *tw* with glue and sprinkle glitter on the glue to make the letters twinkle.

Using **PM** Books Together

Alphabet Blends and Digraphs *sw* Focus on words that have *-w* blends in the initial position.

Using the *Blends and Digraphs* Activity Masters

Dot-to-Dot
For additional practice with /tw/*tw*, engage children in the **manipulative** activity on page 15.

Games and Puzzlers
To reinforce any letter/sound relationship, invite children to select one of the **interactive** ideas on pages 29–32.

 performance assessment opportunities

 projects for *portfolios*

wh *as in whistle*

Show how sounds are blended together to form words and how leaving out or adding a letter changes the word. Use letter cards to build words: *heel, hale, hen, heat, hip.* Read the words. Then change each word by adding letter card *w* in the initial position. Read the new words.

Developing Phonemic Awareness

Read the Rhyme
- Read the rhyme "A whine about whistling," emphasizing the sound of the digraph *wh* in the initial positions.
- Chant words *whine, whistling, whistle, whistles.* Discuss how the words are alike.

Find the Sound
- Show how the /hw/ sound is made in the mouth.
- **(A)** Find something in the room whose name begins with /hw/ like *whistling.* Provide clues such as: change /f/ in *feel* to /hw/, and what do you have? (*wheel*); change /s/ in *sale* to /hw/, and what do you have? (*whale*)

Developing Print Awareness

Identify the Digraph
- Write *whistle* on the chalkboard and ask children to identify the letters that stand for the beginning sound. Confirm that letters *wh* stand for the sound /hw/.
- Reread the rhyme "A whine about whistling" and have children name the words they see that begin with the *wh* digraph.

Find the Digraph
- **In the book** • Make the sound /hw/ as the letters *wh* are traced on page 1 in the book. Read the book together, looking at pictures and emphasizing /hw/ as you read the words.
- **(A)** **Share a rhyme** • Volunteers can hold up the picture in the book as its name is said in the rhyme. Use the rhyme to focus on words that begin with the digraph *wh*.

> Wh *starts* wheelbarrow
> *for carrying heavy loads,*
> *a ferris* wheel *that goes and goes,*
> *and a* whistle *that blows,*
> *the* whiskers *on a great fat cat,*
> *and the webbed wings of a wild* white *bat.*

- Copy the rhyme onto chart paper. Read the rhyme together and underline words that begin with *wh*. Ask children to match each *wh* word in the rhyme with that in the book.
- Find additional words beginning with *wh* in print in the room. Read the words together to confirm that the /hw/ sound begins each word.

The Wheels on the Bus
by Raffi (Crown, 1988)
Children will want to join in this popular song about a bus with wheels that go round and round.

Whale Song
by Tony Johnston (G. P. Putnam's, 1987)
A song-story using numbers as the whale's song.

Whiff, Sniff, Nibble, and Chew:
The Gingerbread Boy Retold
by Charlotte Pomerantz
(Greenwillow, 1984)
Children will enjoy the wordplay and silliness of this version of an old tale.

Exploring Letter/Sound Relationships

Explore Together

Ⓐ • Buddy-read the *wh* book with a partner, identifying words that begin with /hw/*wh*.

• **Feed the whale** • Write words inside a large whale shape on the chalkboard: *wet, whale, watch, wheel, when, window, what, why, worms, whip, white, wave, whiskers, whisper, web, windmill*. Read the words together. Volunteers can find words that begin with /hw/*wh* and draw small fish shapes around them. Count the number of tiny fish the whale has inside it.

• Recite the rhymes on right with children to reinforce the /hw/ sound. Encourage children to write their own rhymes and poems.

Ⓐ • **Giant digraph banner** • Write large letters *wh* on chart paper for children to draw and write words that begin with the digraph *wh*. Display the banner and use as a resource for writing.

Explore on Your Own

Ⓐ • Provide blank whale-shape books for children to draw and write words with initial digraph /hw/*wh*. Tell children to use the digraph banner to think of words to write in their books.

Poems, Rhymes, and Jingles

White whales whip and
whirl their tails.

Wheeler White whistles
while he whittles.

Whisky, frisky,
hippity hop,
Up he goes to the treetop!
Whirly, twirly,
'round and 'round,
Down he scampers
to the ground.
What is it? [squirrel]

Using Ⓟⓜ Books Together

Alphabet Blends and Digraphs *sh, ch, th, ph*
Focus on words that have a variety of -*h* digraphs in the initial position.

At the zoo
(Starters One)
Look for animals with whiskers!

Using the *Blends and Digraphs* Activity Masters

Whistle While You Work *and* Digraph Dominoes
For additional practice with /hw/*wh*, engage children in the **manipulative** activities on pages 19 and 22–23.

Games and Puzzlers
To reinforce any letter/sound relationship, invite children to select one of the **interactive** ideas on pages 29–32.

 performance assessment opportunities

 projects for *portfolios*

Crossword grid

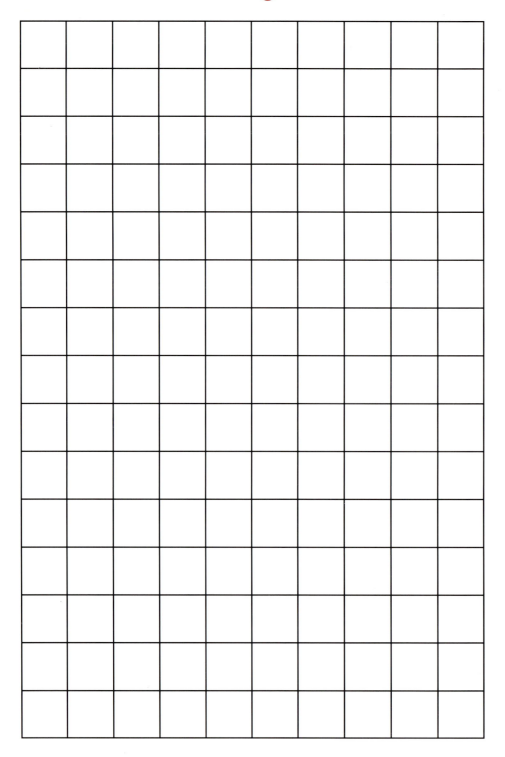

Here is a grid to make crossword puzzles for words that begin with any blend or digraph.

Blend and digraph clusters